A
Confident,
Dynamic
You

∞

Virginia Sanders

Women of Confidence

SERIES

A Confident, Dynamic You

*Ten Keys to Moving from
I Can't to I Can*

MARIE CHAPIAN

VINE BOOKS

SERVANT PUBLICATIONS
ANN ARBOR, MICHIGAN

Vine Books is an imprint of Servant Publications especially designed to serve evangelical Christians.

The names and characterizations in this book are fictional, although based on real events. Any similarity between the names and characterizations and real people is unintended and purely coincidental.

Poetry adapted from *His Thoughts Toward Me*, 1987; *Making His Heart Glad*, 1989; *His Gifts to Me*, 1988, Bethany House Publishers. Used by permission.

All Scripture quotations, unless indicated, are taken from the HOLY BIBLE, NEW INTERNATIONAL VERSION®, © 1973, 1978, 1984 by International Bible Society. Used by permission of Zondervan Publishing House. All rights reserved.

The "NIV" and "New International Version" trademarks are registered in the United States Patent and Trademark Office by International Bible Society. Use of either trademark requires the permission of International Bible Society.

Published by Servant Publications
P.O. Box 8617
Ann Arbor, Michigan 48107

98 99 00 10 9 8 7 6 5 4 3 2

Printed in the United States of America
ISBN 1-56955-037-9

LIBRARY OF CONGRESS CATALOGING-IN-PUBLICATION DATA

Chapian, Marie
A confident, dynamic you : ten keys to moving from I can't to I can / Marie Chapian.
    p. cm — (Women of confidence series ; 1)
ISBN 1-56955-037-9
1. Women—Religious life.   2. Confidence—Religious aspects—Christianity.
I. Title.   II. Series.
BV4527.C42   1997
248.8'43—dc21   97-27773
                                                          CIP

For Christa and Liza

∞

∞

If confidence were a sound, its concert would produce a work of majestic beauty, inspiring awe, wonder, and respect.

If confidence were a work of art, it would glow, it would radiate with color and movement. It would dazzle and thrill the heart as well as the eye.

If confidence lived in you, heaven's thoughts would visit the world.

Marie Chapian

∞

Contents

Introduction

It's a Promise!

∞

The promise of "a confident and dynamic you" sounds almost like something out of a fairy tale, like empty motivational rah-rah with no basis other than enthusiasm. The word "dynamic" is almost too much to take. Nevertheless—every word I share with you in this book is true; its promises are yours to possess. You *can* live a more dynamic and confident life filled with new energy and resolve. You *can* travel through life loving the magic and joy of each day. I offer the Ten Keys in this book to unlock the negative strongholds in your life. These ten keys are road maps and guides for your journey to a confident, dynamic life.

When I was asked by my publisher what I considered the ten most urgent needs in the lives of women in our modern age, I responded, "Don't you mean the *hundred* most urgent needs?" Narrowing this book down to *Ten* Keys to a confident and dynamic life seemed like an impossible task. But as I have traveled in my work, speaking at women's conferences and seminars, interviewing and just talking with women, I have discovered that of the hundreds of "keys," there are definitely ten vital keys necessary to our leading dynamic and confident lives. I believe these Ten Keys will indeed lead us from "I Can't" to "I Can" because I've seen their results in countless lives. This book is the result of twenty years of research, writing, and working with women and women's problems.

The "I Can't" Mentality

The "I Can't" mentality stretches from an innocuous "I can't help myself" to a grim "I can't go on living." "I Can't" creates years of misery and leaves a trail of destruction culminating in sorrow and regret. It is a powerful mindset.

In my years of counseling women from a wide variety of lifestyles and from various cultures around the world, I have seen how this prevailing and cunning "I Can't" mentality so often goes unidentified. It may be called by other names in the vast vocabulary classifications of neuroses, but what it comes right down to is that we women suffer terribly from a *lack of confidence.*

Even a Christian woman can stumble and fall when the answers to the pain and struggle of life aren't immediately forthcoming. She may bravely carry on like a wounded soldier, valiantly swinging her arms in a losing battle, or she may come up with temporary solutions to her problems, which only meet with defeat. She may never stop to wonder whose war she's fighting or why—until one day her "I Can'ts" will be so multiplied that she finally just wears out.

When we don't stop to challenge the deadly hold "I Can't" has on our lives, we continually meet with depression, frustration, misdirected anger, and feelings of uselessness.

Can you punch your way out? An "I Can't" mentality always settles for second-, third- or one hundredth-best. It is a pinched, fearful way of life. It's a sad fact, but it is rare to find any woman who has punched her way out of her fears by taking full spiritual authority over the destructive influences and choices of "I Can't" thinking. An "I Can't" mentality can kill us.

As Christian women, our soul's passion is profoundly linked to our quest for oneness with God. We long for deep, confident spirituality. We want to be strong, capable, and good. We want to enjoy the blessings of life and we want to bless others. We want to lead fulfilling lives and make our world a better place. We also want answers to problems when they arise. We want cures for our pain. We want to abolish inner turmoil. We want solutions for our unhappiness.

With an "I Can't" mentality, a woman may believe disillusionment is part of the normal Christian life. She may even leave the faith entirely, thinking she could do better on her own without religious limitations. She becomes tired of religious rites, laws, and black-and-white definitions of evil and good. She is impatient with God and *his* will. She wants to know why her life isn't working out the way *she* wants it to.

The inspired words of God are brighter than sunlight to our souls. If they are not eclipsed by our own self-sabotaging words, they penetrate all human barriers to create in us the very reflection of God himself. In this renewed state, we have confidence in *him* and his plan for our lives. Therefore, we gain confidence in ourselves as we live our lives in, through, and for him alone.

This book will search out many of the reasons we sabotage our chances to lead truly dynamic lives. It doesn't matter what your circumstances are right now, or what they have been, you can go from "I Can't" to "I Can." You can be a woman of confidence, and your life can change.

The Lazarus Woman

The story of Lazarus being raised from the dead in the eleventh chapter of the Gospel of John is the image used throughout this book. God's urgent desire is for women to "come forth" into new life. The story of Lazarus speaks directly to us as women today. Here's a look at the story:

Once there was a man who lived with his sisters in a village called Bethany. He was a good man and a close friend of Jesus. One day Lazarus became deathly ill. His sisters, Mary and Martha, were very worried about their brother and sent for Jesus to come quickly. The sisters knew Jesus performed miracles and could heal their beloved brother of his sickness.

But Lazarus died before Jesus arrived. In fact, Lazarus had been dead for four days before Jesus arrived in Bethany. At that time it was a common belief that when a person died, the soul remained close by for three days in the hope of returning to the body. For Lazarus, therefore, it appeared that all hope was gone that his life could possibly be restored to him. Lazarus was dead indeed. The tomb where he lay wrapped in linen grave clothes would already be foul-smelling.

When Jesus arrived, Martha immediately assailed him in her sorrow, "If you had just gotten here sooner, my brother wouldn't have died!" But then she drew back and added, "I know that even now God will give you whatever you ask."

Martha's statement was one of hope, and what's more, it was built on confidence. I *know*, she said.

Mary, the other sister, was in the house mourning for her brother, along with many friends and neighbors, when Martha told her Jesus wanted to see her. She rushed out of the house, the others following, to find Jesus. Mary, too, cried out, "Lord, if you had been here, my brother would not have died."

The air was dark with grief, and Jesus saw the agony surrounding the mourners. He was deeply moved in his spirit and asked where the body lay. He, too, wept.

The dead body of Lazarus had been laid in a cave tomb, and a huge stone had been placed across the door. Jesus stood before it and said, *"Take away the stone."*

The response to such a request was one of stunned disbelief. Martha protested, "But, Lord, by this time there is a bad odor! He's been dead four days!"

Jesus answered, simply and plainly, *"Did I not tell you that if you believed, you would see the glory of God?"*

Only God could raise the dead. Jesus knew that. But did everyone else? Did they all really understand who he was? Did they really understand what he had come on earth to accomplish? Did they know the power of love?

Jesus knew exactly what his purpose on earth was. He prayed, *"Father, I thank you that you have heard me. I know that you always hear me."* Divine confidence. Perfect and complete confidence.

The stone was pushed away from the door, and Jesus stood near it and shouted, *"LAZARUS, COME FORTH!"*

Astounding, glorious words.

In a shocking instant, there was a stirring. The dead man must have bolted upright in the tomb, startled by the stink of his own rotting body. The words jerked him to his feet, as though he had been struck by an electric current. He took a step.

"Come out!"

"Lazarus is alive! He was dead and now he is alive!" His loved ones unwrapped him from the strips of linen he had been buried in. "Lazarus is alive!"

Today the voice of Jesus can still be heard at the door of the cave. He is calling us today,

"Come out of your tomb!"

The difference between us and Lazarus is that he did not create his tomb. We, however, make our *own* tombs.

In preparation for writing this book I conducted a "For Women Only" survey with over a thousand women across the country. The women volunteered to take part in the survey, and their responses were anonymous. I share some of their responses in this book. The survey, which appears at the end of the book, proved to me our vital need to learn to become Lazarus Women.

At the root of much of our pain are the untruths we believe to be true. Dark, destructive thoughts that are based on misconceptions and empty lies persist in our minds. These painful thoughts are like little deaths.

In the book *Telling Yourself the Truth,* which I wrote with William Backus, we introduce what we call "misbeliefs." I thank Dr. Backus for coining the expression. Misbeliefs are the perceptions, ideas, thoughts, and words we tell ourselves until we hold them as beliefs, yet they are distorted thoughts not based on truth at all. You will learn to recognize these as you read through each of the Dynamic Keys.

Our souls long to be blessed and lifted up. God is calling us out of our little foul-smelling tombs where we fester in our skewed thoughts. God is empowering us to come forth as the women he designed and ordained us to be in today's age.

A gift of chocolate. Nelson Mandela was in prison for twenty-seven years. Once a year the prisoners received a treasured treat of chocolate. When he received his chocolate, Nelson Mandela didn't eat it but saved the rare sweet to give to a fellow prisoner months later for the man's birthday. This story of self-sacrifice became the topic of discussion with a few friends recently. "What do you think gave Mandela such self-control?" I was asked. "What do you think he had that others don't have?"

"The dynamic of confidence," I answered.

The dynamic of confidence is like great music. It can't be faked. If we try to fake confidence, sooner or later our imitation will deteriorate into ill-placed, discordant notes. You can't share your chocolate, your music, or your truest self without confidence.

Discover the Ten Keys to a confident and dynamic life and lift your soul above the ordinary. I long for every woman to rise up a Lazarus Woman, leaving her "I Can'ts" in the tomb.

How to Use This Book

Each of the Ten Keys in this book has been carefully illustrated from true-life experiences. I want to thank the generous women who have given me their kind permission to use their stories. I have changed the names, but their stories are real.

Read this book one Dynamic Key at a time and then, when you have finished, fill in the questionnaire at the end. Take your time as you read through each Dynamic Key. Underline or circle the passages that especially stand out to you. Reread chapters and think about them. Some of my readers have told me a good idea they have used with other of my books: they transcribe these marked passages onto index cards or into their notebook or current journal to refer to often.

If we take hold of these Ten Keys to a confident and dynamic life, I believe we will become testimonies of the transformation from "I Can't" to "I Can." We will shine with a brightness the whole world will sit up and recognize as the work of God.

These Dynamic Keys are not built on ego and self-vaunting. The Ten Dynamic Keys are not founded on motivational tactics where we repeat positive aphorisms and phrases without a godly foundation. The Dynamic Keys are based on the living and powerful Word of God. They will help us see ourselves with new eyes. They are designed to help us change our self-defeating perceptions of God and the world around us.

I pray that within these pages you will discover your own life reflected and see how very dear you are to the Lord Jesus. I pray you will see how he treasures your life—every detail of it—and how he longs to build in you a dynamic of confidence that cannot be shaken. Preeminently, I long for you to hear the loving voice of God and to throw open all the gates of your heart and soul to follow his wondrous call to *come forth*. My prayer is that you will enter a beautiful new place of love, solitude, hope, courage, fullness, confidence, achievement, creativity, physical strength, and the miracle of multiplying the beauty of who you've become.

> *The woman who hopes in the Lord*
> *will renew her strength.*
> *She will soar on wings like eagles;*
> *She will run and not grow weary,*
> *She will walk and not faint.*
>
> ISAIAH **40:31** *(Paraphrased)*

Part One

∞

Hearing the Promise

The Dynamic of Love

∞

> I have loved you with an everlasting love;
> I have drawn you with loving-kindness.
>
> JEREMIAH 31:3

How do you define love? Can you and I say we *know* love? One person tells me love is putting other people before oneself. Someone else tells me love is giving until it hurts. One woman told me, tongue in cheek, that she believed love was not worrying about whether she was loved or not. Then she added, "I don't think about it. It's too painful."

I've asked women everywhere how they think about themselves in the light of love. Most of the answers I receive to this question are determined by the level of affection these women feel within their familial or friendship frameworks. Depending upon how favorably their relationships are going now or have gone in the past, the answers will vary from "I feel very much loved" to "I have never felt loved in my life."

When I ask about experiencing *God's* love, the answers are almost always the same. Out of countless Christian audiences around the world, very few women (or men) have told me they experience *God's* love every day, or that they think of themselves as uniquely special and important to God. The conclusion seems to be that we look more to people for love than to God—who is the author of love.

"Oh, sure, I know God loves me," a woman will tell me. "The Bible says that God loves me. I just don't feel it."

If we view God's love through a filter of human love, how can we know what his love is really like? Surely it is bigger and better than the faulty human version with which we are so familiar. God's love is not human love. His love is far greater than we can imagine with our finite minds.

Forever I'll Love You

First of all, God loves us with an *everlasting* love. He does nothing in our lives that is not for our good. His very nature is love. His personality, character, and actions are all love. God's nature is not only based on love, it *is* love. God is the source of love.

The faithfulness and love of God surpass human knowledge. We often use the word "love" to describe mere enjoyment, simple affection, compassion, and romantic attraction, so the true meaning of love eludes us. Let's take a closer look at true love—God's love.

Human or divine love? God's love is not moonlight and violins. No, it's not *eros*, self-gratifying romantic love. It is not even the kind of love that exists between good friends or between parents and children, *philia* love. It is not the companionable love of husband and wife. All of these loves are precious and have their place in our human experience. But the love of God, *agape* love, transcends them all. *Agape* love is unselfish, sacrificial love. It is the love we cannot live without if we are going to make sense out of the other kinds of loves. It is love that is supernatural, ever-present, all-encompassing, glorious, life-giving, revitalizing, captivating; it transcends everything and makes possible all human affection.

God is love (1 John 4:8, 16). When God speaks of himself as love, he not only includes his love for you and me, but also his love for all that he has created—time, space, energy, and eternity. God's love is not an illusion or an idea. It is a reality. It is the powerful, divine force that sustains us and draws us to him.

God's love is personal. God loves *you*. He began loving you before you were conceived. He loves you this moment. He will never stop loving you. God has promised we will be loved forever, that there is no shifting or changing of his love.

Romeo or Santa Claus? Three attributes of God are omnipotence, omniscience, and omnipresence. God possesses infinite power (omnipotence), God has perfect and complete knowledge (omniscience), and God is present everywhere (omnipresence). Imagine for a moment that God possessed infinite power without love. Imagine that he had perfect and complete knowledge without love. Imagine he was everywhere, in all things, but without love. He would not be God. All the attributes of God are founded on his primary claim, *"God is love."*

We often think of God's love for us in terms of what he does for us, the prayers he answers, the blessings he bestows upon us. When a prayer is fulfilled, we are certain he loves us. But when he does not answer our prayers in the way we want him to, we're not so sure of his love.

Have you noticed there are pleas he does not respond to immediately? Have you observed there are decisions he makes without us? Has it been your experience that when you pray diligently and faithfully for a certain move on God's part and it doesn't happen, you feel somehow neglected, cheated?

Our problem is that we think of the Lord as Romeo or Santa Claus. We want him to jump in and undo the bad we have created on the earth and for ourselves. These are childish, uneducated notions. God is love—limitless, everlasting love—extended toward all of us.

Desperate!

A friend of mine who is very active in Alcoholics Anonymous telephoned to tell me of an AA meeting she was going to attend to hear a special speaker. I asked her what it was she especially liked about the speaker.

"She talks about being on the very bottom," my friend answered. "She talks about what it's like to be desperate and have no choice but to cry out to God."

Desperate. My friend knows how important it is to be reminded of our condition. So many of us do not know how desperate we are for the love of God. Desperation is not just being at the end of one's rope. Desperation hides under far more subtle trappings. Under what appears to be a good life, we often harbor unrecognized desperation. We need God, but we misunderstand who he is.

God continually draws us with his love. He demonstrates his love to us every day in the natural things of the world and by his endless mercy. He wants us to realize how desperate we are for him and his love. We need to realize that even when our lives seem to be going along smoothly, we are desperately in need.

Lazarus, in his tomb, was beyond the point of desperation. He couldn't even cry out for help. I meet a lot of people who are as "dead" as Lazarus even though they are still walking around. Jesus stands at the door of their dark places and calls out to them, "Come forth!" This may be the most beautiful sound any of us will ever hear. It is the beginning of our new life, of our being truly alive. Key #1, the Dynamic of Love, begins with the realization of our desperation.

I have been a Christian since I was a child. I don't have a memory of a time when I did not know the Lord Jesus as the Son of God. In addition to taking me to dancing and acting lessons as a child, my mother took me to church and Sunday School. I gave my heart to God completely and made Jesus the Lord of my life at the age of twelve. As I grew up, I continued to go to church, to pray, and to read my Bible. But I was also passionately dedicated to my career in the theater. It was my life.

At seventeen, I was studying and performing in New York. I believed God's love and blessings depended completely upon my doing a good job and giving my all to my work. I thought I was putting the Lord first in my life by denying myself the pleasures other girls my age enjoyed. I spent almost every waking hour of the day in dance classes, voice lessons, and acting classes. I wanted to please God with the gifts he had given me. I believed his love was something to be earned. I believed that the harder I worked and the better I became at my art, the more deserving of God's love and acceptance I would be. When all went well, I believed it to be a sign of God's blessing and approval. I was dependent upon media reviews that praised my work because these fueled my sense of identity and told me that my work had value and meaning.

This attitude is not unusual. I have met countless women and men who spend their lives *earning* God's approval. Without knowing it, I had limited God and his love for me. I was desperate and didn't know it. I was desperate to know God for who he really was, not for who I thought he was.

"Come Forth!"

Many women have a career-oriented relationship with God. If things go well, if our expectations and demands are met, we have a sense of gratification. We feel God is close to us. Many women are content with this level of living, never thirsting to know God for the happiness and meaning he gives us. We never get desperate for God.

What happens when events, circumstances, and situations run amok? What happens when the career spirals downward? What happens when demands go unmet, expectations are unfulfilled, things go horribly wrong? We may feel that God is somehow against us, or that he wanted to bless someone else more than he wanted to bless us with what we prayed for. Depression, physical symptoms of stress, intense anxiety, anger at God, and even acts of violence can result.

Imagine for a moment that you are stripped of everything dear to you. Your family is gone, your house is gone, your friends have fled. You've lost your job and are without an income. Everything you own and everyone dear to you has suddenly evaporated into thin air. What do you have now? *Who are you now?*

Only one Person will remain when all else fails. He stands before you saying, "Come forth!" Do you hear him? Realizing the depth of our poverty makes us able to hear him. Desperation makes us completely dependent upon God. In our desperation, we say to God, "*You* define my personhood. *You* make of me what you will. Let my life be a glory to you."

When I was at the height of my theatrical career, I felt a deep spiritual restlessness. Even though my future looked rosy and I wasn't particularly unhappy, I was desperate and ready to admit it. I said to God, "There must be more to being a Christian. I must be missing something."

I began to understand that God wanted *all* of me, not just what I could *do.* He wanted me to know him in a far deeper way than I had imagined. My prayers then became, "Lord, guide me, show me, teach me, lead me." This meant listening to him. I wasn't used to listening. I was used to doing most of the talking.

The first step in the Key of Dynamic Love is to realize your desperation. The second step is to *give God the opportunity to lovingly speak to you.*

I believe a life without the knowledge of God's love is like life in a tomb. The air in the tomb is fetid. Without the living experience of God's love, our lives are uninspired; we do not have the aroma of heaven's wisdom and joy. Without God's revitalizing love, we are incapable of breathing life's pure lovely air of confidence. Without the motivating force of his love, we can be very busy people, but we are dead without even being aware of it.

When Jesus called to Lazarus, he came forth because death couldn't hold him. And when Jesus Christ calls you, death can't hold you, either. You won't stay in that tomb. You'll "come forth."

It is love that calls you today. It is God's loving-kindness that summons you out of your dark tomb of fear, despair, and confusion.

Power in the Word. Resurrection—coming forth from the tomb of our own making—begins with his Word. Careful, decisive study of his Word teaches us to hear and recognize his voice as nothing else possibly could.

The first chapter of the Gospel of John tells us, "In the beginning was the Word, and the Word was with God, and the Word was God. He was with God in the beginning" (Jn 1:1-2).

The Word is a word conceived and a word uttered. It is the substance and essence of God. The living manifestation and expression of himself was given to us by his Word—Jesus Christ. "The Word became flesh and made his dwelling among us" (Jn 1:14). God makes his mind known to us through his written Word.

Listening to the truth of God's Word, meditating constantly on that truth, and speaking it out loud to yourself increases your love relationship with God. The love the Lord has for you as a woman becomes clearer as you soak your mind in the Word of God and listen for his voice. He gently guides you out of the trappings of a desperate life.

This is an every-day process. The time spent reading the Word of God, memorizing his words, and meditating on them are critical to your walking in the confidence you were born to possess.

When we allow God's love to permeate our conscious minds and actions we learn to see ourselves through his eyes, the eyes of love. Every remaining moment in your life depends upon your ability to see yourself as a loved woman. You are loved perfectly and wholly by God. When his love pours through your being, you find how capable you are of loving him back. "The love of God has been poured out in our hearts by the Holy Spirit who was given to us" (Rom 5:5, NKJV).

The source of all love is God. In order to use the Key of Dynamic Love in the door of your heart, you must receive Jesus Christ as your Savior. He became flesh for you. And he gave himself on the cross so that, in a miraculous way, the Holy Spirit of God might be infused into you.

Jesus Christ is God's gift of love to you. Without this salvation experience, you will find that you cannot rise up out of your desperation. You will not be able to hear his voice clearly. Jesus said that no one can see the kingdom of God unless he or she is born again (see John 3:3).

Are You Lovable?

In the "For Women Only" survey I conducted, I asked the question "When do you feel most lovable?" Here is just a sampling of the answers:

I feel most lovable—

- when I am skinny.
- when my house is perfect.
- when my family does something unexpected to show me they love me.
- when my kids hug me and love me unconditionally.
- when I'm able to make others smile.
- when I'm thin and taking good care of myself.
- never.
- when I'm serving others.

- when I have a cheerful, loving attitude.
- when I'm twenty pounds lighter.
- when I'm not in a rush and my house is clean.
- when I'm held and cuddled (which is never now).
- when I'm being funny.

Not one woman in a thousand said, "I *always* feel lovable." There were many responses of a spiritual nature, such as "I feel lovable when I'm alone with God" or "I feel lovable when I remember Jesus loves me unconditionally." But not one response came back expressing the truth that we are utterly and completely lovable every second of our lives, awake or asleep, for better or worse, because of the simple promise that God has chosen to love us unconditionally and everlastingly.

"I have loved you with an everlasting love" (Jer 31:3).

Lazarus was called from the tomb of death by the power of love. The miracle was not due to anything Lazarus did or felt. He wasn't raised from the dead because the tomb was sparkling clean or because he was thin and wearing his nice new grave clothes. Do you get it? He didn't do anything to earn God's love—and neither do we.

Life without God's love is like Lazarus' dark tomb. How can we breathe the pure sweet air of confidence if nothing in us is inspired by love? What can possibly inspire us if not love? Heaven's wisdom demands that we open ourselves to being loved by God.

Does God like girls as much as boys? When I was Junior Church Director in a large church in the Midwest, a little girl came up to me and asked, "Do you think God likes girls as much as boys?" She had a brother whom her parents were extremely proud of. The brother received most of the parents' attention, and since the parents were religious, the little girl figured God liked boys best.

This little girl's confidence was being shaken at an early age. Already she figured being a girl meant she was somehow inferior. Maybe God himself considered her inferior—second rate. What messages from the world around you are you receiving about yourself as a female person?

It's important to realize the influences that give us the impressions we have of ourselves. Many of us are taught to engage in submissive relationships and to be quiet in church, and almost all conversations or sermons abound with "he" or "man" to indicate humankind.

I heard a preacher proudly exclaim from the pulpit on Mother's Day, "I bought flowers for my dear wife today. We've been married twenty-five years and she hasn't missed cooking me a single meal." The woman next to me leaned over and said, "He could hire someone for that job—can't he say anything else nice about her?" In some churches, we are sometimes admonished to put ourselves down as miserable wretches.

From many pulpits both men and women are railed at for what we don't do for God, what sinners we are, how we fail God at every turn, how we should increase our giving, and about how hot the flames of hell are. In the end we're exhausted and filled with anxiety about our Christian walk.

Of course, we fall short of the glory of God—we all do. Men, women, everybody. But God is a forgiving, merciful God. Jesus died on the cross to forgive us our sins and cleanse us of all unrighteousness. He teaches us to concentrate on his goodness and love, and not upon how horrible we have been in our nasty, carnal selves.

Love is far more than following a prescribed list of legalistic

Do's and Don'ts. God's love asks that we come into a place of oneness with him. This we do without a set of rules, contingencies, or threats. I don't mean we should live lawless lives, self-centered and doing as we think best with no basis other than our own whims to guide us. Far from it! Paul writes in Romans 7, "Is the law sin? Certainly not! Indeed I would not have known what sin was except through the law."

To live a confident life is to live within the moral precepts of the Bible. We live lives characterized by Ephesians 4:22, 24: "Put off your old self, which is being corrupted by deceitful desires; ...and ... put on the new self, created to be like God in true righteousness and holiness."

Jesus invites us: "Come!"

The Word of God emphasizes the glorious potential in a Christ-centered life. Freedom is there for the taking. But that freedom from the tomb of defeat depends entirely upon our willingness to accept it.

When God is silent. I have certainly been tested in my decision to enter into the reality of his undying love. There have been times in my life when it has seemed that, outwardly, God was not on my side at all. I have been in situations where I felt no warm assurance from God such as the hug or word of comfort one receives from a human friend. There have been times when I felt none of God's encouragement to go on in trust and faith, and when I didn't have a sweet feeling of his presence and approval. At those times I had to ask myself, "Do I trust my feelings or do I trust God's Word?" I had to plunge myself into his Word and repeat over and over again what he has explained to us, his dear children:

God is love. The woman who lives in love, lives in God and

God in her. In this way, love is made complete among us so that we women will have confidence.

1 JOHN 4:16-17a, paraphrased

(I've taken liberties to personalize the above Scripture. Sometimes that helps us to see in a graphic way how the Scriptures pertain to us personally.)

I want always and forever to see God as he said he is: *love.* I want to maintain this truth whether or not he answers my prayers as I want him to. I've learned that I don't come to him through hard work or achievements. I don't come to him deserving of his love because of anything I have done. I come to him because he loves me and calls me to himself.

Just as he called Lazarus, he cries out, "Come forth," to you and to me. That means moving forward, not backward to the harried and dark place of the past. That means moving forward into a place of life.

I have had much to learn about living in God's love. I have had to learn to see him as being loving in every detail of life. I have learned to pray with honesty, "Thank you, Lord, for your perfect love that fills and guides my life without error. You see me and my life as precious. You care for me as a person of immense value and worth. I am confident in your decisions. I am confident in myself as your loved one. Have your way."

I have had to learn that God doesn't have a designated day when he answers our requests. It's a mistaken notion that God should jump the instant we call. Some women I've spoken to have had the idea that God was like a lover or a kindly old soul who should come to our rescue anytime we are in distress.

A woman told me sadly, "Oh, sure, I know he's the Son of God and he can do anything, but he just doesn't choose to help me in my dilemma. He's just going to allow me to sink and go down the tubes in these problems of mine, I just know it. But praise his holy name anyhow."

Our moments of testing are occasions to stretch our faith and confidence in God's love. We cry out for answers to our problems; we agonize for God to answer our prayers.

And how does God answer?

What?

Nothing. Silence.

We ask him to please speak to us, to please help us to understand why there is so much sorrow and suffering in our world. Why *do* bad things happen to good people?

In the dark, starless hour of pain, we hear ... *silence.*

My Aunt Eleanor was like a second mother to me, and when she died it was a dreadful blow to me, her family, and all who loved her. She was a dynamic Christian woman, dearly and tenderly loved, and her loss seemed so senseless, so unfair. She was still young, vibrant, and filled with the joy of the Lord. But she was stricken with cancer and died. Why? Why didn't God heal her? Why did a good woman who helped so many people die such an untimely death?

Only when embraced by the knowledge that God in his omnipotence, omnipresence, and omniscience knows and sees all things can we begin to accept our lot. God is forever. His love is forever, and the unfairness of the world only makes sense in that context.

He Will Establish You in Love

We must accept the fact that until Jesus returns to establish his kingdom, there will always be sin in the world. Here we are, living in the midst of the world's sin, but his love pulls us out of its cloying tentacles. We are in the world but we are not of it.

Jesus refers to us as the light of the world as long as we are in it. By being transformed in the power of God's love, we begin to learn where *we* fit in this world. Jesus has triumphed over sin, and he came to bind up the brokenhearted, to proclaim liberty and the opening of our prisons to the captives. Again, he speaks:

> I am here to give you a crown of beauty for ashes, to anoint you with the oil of joy for mourning, to place on your shoulders the garment of praise for the spirit of heaviness. You will be called an oak of righteousness, a planting of the Lord for the display of his splendor. ISAIAH 61:3 (paraphrased)

Fear, worry, anxiety, anger, jealousy, all belong in the tomb like the one in which Lazarus was buried. It's time to leave the old, dead things of the past in the tomb and come out into the sunshine of a renewed life in Christ.

Perhaps your mind is quite accustomed to listening to the discrimination and threats of the world around you. Perhaps you have believed these to be more real than the promises of God. All of these false mis-beliefs belong in the tomb, too.

We are continually tempted to slip out of the knowledge of God's love and sabotage ourselves with our old "I Can't" ways. That is why Paul said, "Don't let the world around you squeeze you into its own mold, but let God remake you."

If love were an object you could carry around with you, what would you do with it? Forget it on a store counter like you might a pair of sunglasses? Would you leave it on the dresser along with your watch and loose change? Would you let someone else baby-sit for it? Would you put it in your pocket along with your wallet and key chain? Or would you treasure it and care for it tenderly? Would you keep it in a safe place and spend time every day looking at it, touching it, holding it close to you?

Claiming the Dynamic Key of Love means you will never again take God's love for granted. God's love is much closer to you than an object you can see or carry in your purse. God's love is *within* you.

In the next chapter, the Dynamic Key of Solitude, we will look at the importance of embracing our solitude. We truly hear from God in the place of solitude. He can speak to our hearts there. We know how loved we are when we can hear God's whisper in our ear and when we can see our face in his.

GOD SPEAKS:

I am rich in mercy toward you.

It is My will that you open the eyes

of your heart and see what an incredible quality

of love the Father has given you

through Me.

The Father holds you snugly

in His thoughts with love.

His thoughts and plans for you

are good

and hold glory beyond your dreams.

EPHESIANS 1:18-19; JEREMIAH 29:11

2

The Dynamic of Solitude

∞

Within us is a place where we connect with God, ourselves, and the world around us. It is the secret place of solitude where we can link our souls to the will of God. From this place we go out to meet our social surroundings and the outside world.

There are those of us, women especially, who find it difficult to be alone. We find no enjoyment in solitude. But our souls are never less alone than when we are alone with God. In the secret, inner place of our hearts, in our solitude, we meet God and his unconditional love.

This is an expectant place where confidence is formed like a precious work of art, because there we feel our souls kissed by God. It is there we learn that our confidence is more than a life skill. It is a sacred gift.

How Do You Find Solitude?

By "solitude" I do not mean an ascetic withdrawal from a social world. I'm not saying you should live as a hermit. Solitude is a place in the heart. It is where we live with God. It is that place of divine hearing and knowing, discovered through a hunger for God and his love.

Solitude requires a heart of prayer and a stillness that is devoid of anxiety. We can't hear him when we are continually talking, worrying, begging for something.

Solitude does not depend upon our surroundings. It is not an hour a day set aside for quiet time (although that time can help you learn the way of solitude). It's not the occasional weekend in the woods with your Bible. When I speak of solitude, I am speaking of a state of being. It involves all the days and hours of your life on earth.

I am speaking of silencing your own voice and listening to his as a *way of life*.

Confidence, born in solitude. God calls us to solitude when he gently beckons us to come away with him. In solitude we hear him speak to us of his love. Instead of the winds of turmoil beating against us, we feel the finger of God upon our foreheads, we feel the Holy Spirit breathing sweetness into our veins. We know him and we know we are loved.

The Dynamic Key of Solitude will unlock your soul as will nothing else. When you are alone with your Beloved, your soul emerges clean from the cares of the world. Once you have found solitude within, you carry it with you every day, every moment.

Solitude means withdrawal into God in the depths of your being. In silence and solitude, your individuality is affirmed. You will find strength and healing in the silence where you are completely safe with God. He speaks in a still, small voice, so still and so small it can only be heard in solitude. From that original place of silence you will continue to hear his voice. The activities of your day are energized because your soul is being cared for and nourished continually. You are led by his Spirit as you carry on your life in a world of noise and clatter.

We may fill our lives with spiritual activities, meetings, ministries, and a lot more, yet our souls can still remain hard within us. We may spend time in prayer and in reading the Bible, but still wrestle with lack of understanding. Our souls cry out for attention. They plead for solitude. They become starved from neglect.

I find the Dynamic Key of Solitude so empowering that I can hardly find words to adequately express how truly vital I feel it is to a confident and dynamic life in Christ. Understand this—solitude is more than an absence of sounds, it is an invisible *place* in your heart where you let yourself be molded and transformed by the Spirit of God.

Give a gift to your soul. When a woman tells me she has no time for solitude, I wonder if she is resisting God's still, small voice and the cries of her own soul.

Our souls hunger to be fed. When we are assailed by guilt, fear, pressures to succeed, worry, and concern for others, we tend to put aside the needs of our own souls. The motivation behind our prayer life and Bible study then becomes our many concerns. We only approach God with external needs, and our souls can remain hungry our entire lives.

A woman may come to me beleaguered with worry and fear. She will tell me with a certain hard insistence, "I trust the Lord, I really do. I trust the Lord." I do not doubt her trust, but I can sense the hunger of her soul for the sweet balm of heavenly love. I often suggest to such a woman that she embrace her solitude as a way to bless her soul. I explain that through silence and solitude, she will experience a divine and glorious union with the Lord Jesus in a way that will enrich and nourish her soul and bless the Lord.

Increasingly, her faith will be based on love, which is our first Dynamic Key.

"My soul thirsts for thee," David cried out to the Lord in Psalm 63. David recognized the needs of his soul. To prevent the worries of his demanding life from swamping the still, small voice of God within, he nurtured the integrity of his soul. All the cares of his life melted in the inner solitude where he went to be alone with his God. He wrote, "He makes me lie down in green pastures, he leads me beside quiet waters, he *restores my soul*" (Ps 23: 2-3, italics mine). David's strength came from God, and he obtained that strength in the secret place where he was united with God, his core of integrity. David had learned to love solitude and to meet God in silence during his long years as a shepherd.

We need to learn to nourish our souls as he did. I suggest trying to set aside at least an hour a day for solitude in order that your soul be nourished. In these moments with God, we silence the world and our own noise and concentrate on God and his Word.

This year I spent many hours in silence. The time I spent in solitude was not my regular prayer time or Bible study. I disciplined myself not to speak or pray in these times of solitude but to remain absolutely still. I just listened.

At first, it was difficult. I wanted to move around, talk to the Lord, tell him my thoughts, ask questions. I am a very active person; I wanted to sing, pray, *do* something. But my soul needs me to be quiet and listen. My soul thirsts for God. And so does yours.

Learn to love solitude and silence. Absorb God's love and tenderness as you listen to his still, small voice. Solitude is a glorious gift to your soul.

Is solitude lonely? A young woman pulled me aside at a women's conference and tearfully explained that she had broken up with her boyfriend and her loneliness was almost more than she could bear. What should she do?

In her distraught face, I could see her desperate need to know she was not alone. I explained to her that loneliness is not the same as being alone.

I recommended that the young woman begin to spend one hour a day alone in a time of solitude with God. I told her to concentrate on the nearness of God, his love for her, and how precious her soul was to him. Hesitating, the girl agreed to follow my advice. As I watched her move away into the crowd, I prayed she would hold to her promise.

Six months later I was speaking in another city and a young woman approached me. "Remember me?" she asked happily. I didn't remember her. I didn't recognize her as the same sad woman. "I took your advice, Marie," she told me. "I did what you said to do. I embraced my solitude, and I understand now what you mean. I can tell you in all honesty that now I am alone but not lonely!"

God had met that young woman in a wonderful way. It wasn't activity her soul longed for, or another boyfriend, or busyness to fill her lonely hours. It was God himself. She exemplified David's cry, "As the deer pants for streams of water, so my soul pants for you, O God" (Ps 42:1).

I was thrilled at the transformation of that young woman. We gain confidence through an awareness that we are not alone. In solitude the Lord teaches us what we can learn in no other place. Like the deer, whose life depends upon water, our souls depend upon God's communion with us. God is always available and waiting. We must come to him with waiting, open hearts.

What Is Loneliness?

I visit retirement homes and I see women sitting in chairs, staring at the floor, plucked from active lives they once thought would never end. They may not have a meaningful conversation with another person for days or months at a time. These elderly women depend on strangers to cook their food, make their beds, remind them what day of the week it is. These women, somebody's mother, somebody's daughter, somebody's wife, are now tucked away in a place where the most noticeable feature is the television, broadcasting its message of youth and beauty.

Of course, loneliness doesn't begin in old age. It's a thief which can begin its work early in your life, ready to steal whatever joy you possess at any age. Loneliness is like a heavy coat, a gray, heavy, miserable-fitting thing with fleas and moths nesting in its sleeves. Loneliness says I *can't* help myself. I *can't* change my situation into something beautiful.

Solitude says, I *can* allow God to fill me with his love, wisdom, and companionship. I can feel and know for certain that in Christ I am *never* alone. I can exchange my heavy cloak of loneliness for a brilliant-colored garment threaded with gold and shining like the sun for all to see.

Feelings of loneliness are not sin. They are signs of a thirsting soul. Loneliness tells us it is time to embrace our solitude and hear from God.

Let's look at five people and their lonely circumstances:

- Beatrice is lonely. She lost her husband to cancer two years ago. She still talks to his photograph, kisses his clothes, cries at night.

- Philip is lonely. His wife left him two months ago after twenty years of marriage. He sits at the kitchen table staring at the stack of unpaid bills before him. He has never balanced a checkbook, doesn't know how to cook a chicken, can't make a bed.

- Corrie has moved to a new town. She doesn't know her neighbors. Her relatives are far away. She spends her evenings watching television and binge eating, and wakes up crying every morning from loneliness.

- Helen retired from a teaching job she held for thirty-five years. She joined community service clubs, began ballroom dancing lessons, enrolled in ceramics classes at a junior college, and began writing a memoir. She's active and busy—but Helen still feels lonely.

- Susanna is a woman with three healthy, bright children and a financially successful husband who loves her. She lives in a beautiful home with a stunning view of the Pacific Ocean and the California coastline. She drives a new car, wears designer clothes—and tries to fill up the hours of every day to avoid facing her loneliness.

Beatrice, Philip, Corrie, and Helen have lost someone or something special in their lives. Loss often leads to loneliness. A loved one, a friend, a job, personal possessions, health, are gone and a hole is left inside.

Unlike the other four, Susanna has not lost anything. She is simply bored. In each case, however, David's words "Why are you downcast, O my soul?" (Ps 42:11) are never asked. The soul remains starved for God because its hunger has been ignored.

Many women think they will find God in church life, prayer groups, Christian activities, and a myriad of ministries designed to help others. The answers to their dilemmas of loneliness are sought through social interactions—more or new activities, committees, another group, new friends, more responsibility. Without such social structures, these women experience a collapse in their sense of well-being. They lack inner peace and contentment because they're so busy they don't have time to experience solitude.

Speaking from experience. There are many times in my life when I've felt lonely, but I think traveling has been the loneliest of all. When I first began traveling to other countries, I experienced mixed feelings. On one hand I was enthusiastic and energized, breathless with excitement and wonder, and on the other hand I was homesick and lonely.

I have been in countries where Americans are despised, where women are treated poorly, and where my white skin and blonde hair advertised me as a foreign enemy. I was once questioned by police in a small town in a then-Communist country for taking a walk along the river during the day, when everybody was supposed to be working. But I've found that the intimate presence of God has proven greater than any such trial.

Among primitive tribes in South America and Africa, where much communication is nonverbal, a wrong gesture can cause serious consequences. A missionary friend of mine told me about a tribe of people who considered folding the arms in a certain way to be an indication of evil spirits at work. They believed it required a violent flogging to release the evil spirits from the person. Can you imagine being beaten mercilessly simply for folding your arms?

My friend, writer Julie Brickman, in her essay "Writers with Two Cultures," writes about the loneliness she felt as an American living in Canada. She speaks of the culture shock she experienced in her first months of living in a place that wasn't supposed to be "foreign" and the disdain she felt surrounding her at every step.

"Those Americans," a businessman once said to her, "they come into a roomful of strangers and blab on about themselves. Whatever makes them think we're interested?"

An experience of an American woman writer traveling in an Arab country illustrates loneliness in a dramatic way. The woman had lost her way walking to the train station. She stopped to ask directions of a male shopkeeper. The man abruptly turned his back on her as if she were diseased.

Later, it was explained to the woman that she was an "uncovered woman" doing the unspeakable—making eye contact with a man. To add more shame to the situation, she was *talking* to him. This was what prostitutes did. If he were to answer her, it would mean he was communicating with a prostitute, which would, in turn, label and disgrace him.

The woman had nowhere to turn. She was lost and in need of directions, completely out of place, forsaken except for God, who promises, "Never will I leave you; never will I forsake you" (Heb 13:5). We may feel lonely, but are we truly alone? No. God's promise to be with us is more real than our feelings of loneliness.

When French journalist Jean Dominique Bauby, former editor-in-chief of the French *Elle* Magazine, died in 1997, he left behind an incredible story of courage and passion. Bauby was forty-five in 1995 when he suffered a massive stroke that left him totally paralyzed except for the muscle in his left eyelid. He learned to communicate by a series of blinks representing the letters of the alphabet. By winking, he dictated a 137-page book about his condition, a memoir celebrating life. Unable to swallow, to speak, to touch a loved one, he was trapped in his body. He described his state as being "like a mind in a jar." What could be more lonely?

What impresses me most about Bauby is his love of living, his refusal to give in to the tragedy that had blasted his life. Although he was locked in, he was as alive as you and I are.

Bauby met loneliness head-on and took advantage of that lone-liness to embrace his solitude. His loneliness was transformed into a beautiful coat of gold. *Time* Magazine wrote, "In the end, Bauby's spirit proved stronger than his heart. He died as he had lived: with dignity."

Loneliness won't kill you. But a lack of dignity and courage might. The answer to loneliness is to embrace your solitude.

You Can Embrace Solitude

Our experiences of loneliness pale in the light of such great saints of God like Joan of Arc and the Apostle John. Young Joan was strapped to a post and set on fire, not for folding her arms, but for hearing from God. She was completely alone, undefended. She was a woman of prayer who knew how to embrace solitude and lis-ten as God spoke to her. As she burned to death, all she had left was her soul's union with Christ Jesus. Legend tells us that in the smoldering ashes, her heart remained untouched by the fire.

Let's look at the Apostle John. As an old man he was con-demned to a desolate island to live out his days in exile. On the isle of Patmos, aged, alone, alienated, he was cut off from all human sources of comfort, support, encouragement, and love. How lonely can it get?

Yet it was the Apostle John who wrote, "He that overcometh shall inherit all things" (Rv 21:7). He couldn't stop marveling at the love of God. In fact, John referred to himself as the disciple Jesus loved best, and his writings are second only to the Song of Solomon in their expression of intimacy with God.

John's entire life was a difficult one, filled with trials. He saw

Jesus crucified on the cross and was persecuted by Saul of Tarsus. Under cruel Herod Agrippa, John saw his own brother James slaughtered with the sword. John was persecuted under Domitian, and Tertullian tells how he was hauled off to Rome and cast into an oversized vat of boiling oil. He lived through it all. Though no longer a young man, he was sentenced to hard labor. Then, old and weary, he was condemned and exiled to the isle of Patmos—alone.

On Patmos, the Apostle John wore loneliness as he had worn all his sufferings, like a crown. "It is in silence and solitude that spirits attain their complete beauty," writes F. B. Meyer. In John's solitude he shouted out loud enough for all the ages to hear, "Behold what manner of love the Father has bestowed on us, that we should be called the children of God!" (1 Jn 3:1, NKJV). In the Apostle John we see how, through perfect union with Jesus Christ, loneliness is transformed into sacred solitude.

Years before John wrote from Patmos, Jesus' disciple Stephen endured his last moments on earth. Rocks and stones, hurled by an infuriated mob, rained down upon his head, breaking his bones, splattering his blood, rupturing his body until he could breathe no more. There was nobody there to defend him, rescue him, befriend him. Yet he had developed such a singular closeness to God that he "saw heaven opened," even as he was being killed.

I could fill this book with stories of Christian martyrs. Those men and women who have gone before us, men and women who lived lives of monumental courage and strength for not only their last hours but for most of their lives, suffered *alone*.

Were these heroes of the faith *lonely*? When we embrace our solitude, the place where God lives in us, we cannot be lonely for long. We are alone but not lonely.

Joy in solitude. There is no better answer to the problem of loneliness than hearing the voice of the Lord Jesus and embracing his love for you. Embrace his spirit within you. You can do nothing but love him back, and in loving him back, you accept and love yourself. Now you can reach out and touch your world.

To embrace your solitude means to be truly content with yourself. Solitude teaches contentment as does no other experience in life. One of the greatest gifts you can give yourself is to spend more time alone with God. When you're lonely and feeling bad, embrace your solitude. Withdraw from the noise of life to be quiet with God. Solitude can only be reached by being in a state of openness and quiet. If we're not accustomed to it, it takes time to settle into that state, but once we do, the world becomes a different place. From the place of solitude, you see life with new eyes.

In that place, God looks at you and you look at him. When you come away, others can see the face of God in you. Joy overtakes your gloom, satisfies your hungry soul, meets your needs. You will have a joy that cannot be taken away because you have found it in the unshakable place where God inhabits you.

Jesus himself suffered and died on the cross—alone, desolate. In one horrible moment he was swallowed up in all the loneliness of humankind. He agonized, "My God, why have you forsaken me?" By enduring that moment, he erased our separation from God. For our sakes, to pay the price of human sin, he experienced the anguish of complete alienation. No loss, separation, alienation, or rejection on earth can ever match the desolation of that moment. Through his crucifixion, Jesus not only experienced the ultimate loneliness, he also guaranteed to all who believe in him that we need never be left alone again. Now he is always with us.

The Holy Spirit of God fuses with our spirits the instant we open ourselves to the wholeness of God by inviting the Savior,

Jesus Christ, into a place of prominence in our souls. We give ourselves completely to God through his Son, and from this union we develop into our truest selves. Through this union we learn and experience true confidence.

When you spend time in solitude, you can identify your sin more clearly and nail it to the cross of Jesus. You can see more easily how your neediness has bred self-destructive urges. You can sort out the hurtful messages you give yourself and receive God's help to change them.

Is it possible to go through life without doing any of this? Certainly. Just as a marble-top table can stand in the hallway year after year, its cool surface always remaining the same—so is the empty, Spirit-starved soul able to go on just being. We might say, "I'm just being *me*," but we lack the divine luster that only God's Spirit can provide.

I don't want to be stone-cold, and neither do you. Let's proceed on the glorious adventure of discovery, renewal, and growth.

GOD SPEAKS:

To become silent before Me
is to release control
   over your own life and destiny.
Your true life is in the silent interior
   of your heart
     where you must learn to live.
The world of your senses is not a sufficient guide.
   Yes, I am in the mountains and the oceans,
birds and beasts, flowers and fruits,
   deserts and plains—
   all of which I created with a word...
But your soul is the home of My spirit.
   Listen there for My quiet voice.
   Leave your noisy plans
be still in the fiery gaze of My love,
   even as Moses stood before the burning bush.
Come to the secret, inner home in your heart
where I speak to you lovingly
   in silence.

3

The Dynamic of Hope

∞

Hope is the confident expectation of God's best for us. It is confidence in the power and wisdom of his loving heart: the confident expectation of the mighty move of his hand on our behalf. Hope is not passive; it is active and believing.

We say words like "I hope I get that job I applied for," and what we're saying is "I want that job I applied for." Sometimes we say things like "I hope we get there on time," or "I hope it doesn't rain," or "I hope you have a nice day." But none of these statements has much to do with the actual meaning of hope.

Hope is not a belief that says "I'll get what I want if I just hang on long enough." True hope is more than waiting for answered prayer or better circumstances. It believes that God will prevail in the face of what seem to be impossible circumstances. Hope walks hand-in-hand with vision.

My definition of hope is this:

> Hope is the process of jumping from one place to another. We jump with our needs toward God in complete confidence, knowing we will land safely in the loving arms of his answer.

∞

Hope is more than mere words. In troubled times, words offered to encourage us, comforting words such as "Don't give up," "You can do it," "Have faith," and "Hang in there," bounce off our souls. To really help us in the face of pain and suffering, we need more than a pep talk. We need hope.

Hope is a gift from God. None of us can manufacture it. It stares seemingly hopeless circumstances in the face with a confidence that is born not from some inner determination but from the assurance of God's Word. He says he will never leave us nor forsake us. God gave this gift to Job of old, who said, "Though he slay me, yet will I trust him" (Jb 13:15, KJV). He gives the same gift to us. Hope is the spark within us that says, "Even though I am suffering, let's see what God will do." Hope makes us able to take the risk of faith. It motivates us to plunge blindly onward, our hand locked tightly in the Lord's.

Some of us never taste hope. We have resigned ourselves to grimly endure life. Even Christians, glib with words of faith, often lack the gift of hope. To be one who not only endures but prevails in the face of life's onslaughts with confidence and energy, it is imperative to find a hopeful vision. For without it we will perish.

His Gifts: Faith, Hope, Love

"And now these three remain, faith, hope and love" (1 Cor 13:13). This chapter of the Bible is about love. Dropped, however, into the last verse of the chapter are two new words: "faith" and "hope." Just what is this hope named here? How is it different from faith? How do faith and hope relate to love?

Faith encourages hope. "Faith is being sure of what we hope for and certain of what we do not see" (Heb 11:1). *Faith* is the solid, unflinching belief in his Word and promises. Faith provides the proof and conviction of unseen reality. With it we are completely certain of what we do not yet see; we perceive as fact that which is not revealed to the senses. With faith assuring us, our hope can help us leap confidently across the valleys of uncertainty.

Love wraps around both faith and hope. It is the assurance that God hears us and cares about every detail of our lives. That is enough to give anyone hope!

How do you nourish hope? Hope requires us to have a vision. Hopeful vision gives us a certain kind of spiritual athleticism to jump beyond the ordinary and the obvious to that which is eternal. Without a specific vision, hope remains too vague and distant to be of any practical assistance.

To find a hopeful vision, enter your solitude and allow the embrace of God to keep you quiet. At the foot of the cross, lay your suffering, your job opportunity, your illness, or whatever else seems hopeless. Tell God in silence and confidence that you trust him, that your hope is in him and in his overriding wisdom. Acknowledge that you don't know how to hope correctly for things or situations, because hope is God's gift to you. His gift of hope gives you a confident expectation of his best for you. Ask him to guide you, show you, give you that hope.

I use David's words in Psalms 42:5 to talk to my own soul: "My soul,... put your hope in God." I make the words of Psalms 119:74 my own prayer: "I have put my hope in your word."

With my Bible in my hand, I read with new eyes. God's Word develops hope in the depths of my soul.

Let me tell you the story of some women who struggled with life because they did not have a hopeful vision.

I spoke at an all-day seminar in a church where the women in attendance seemed to have the grimmest faces I'd ever seen. I thought maybe someone had died and they were all in mourning. Their spirits seemed heavy-burdened, their faces hard.

At the snack break between sessions, as I listened to their conversations and talked with them, I began to discover the reason for their dour expressions. They had faith all right—the white-knuckled kind of faith that whooped and shouted at God. It was a faith devoid of hope.

Without the understanding of how precious and loved we are, we can't have hope. These women knew how to beg, how to pound the walls of heaven, how to pray without ceasing. They knew how to "give the Lord no rest." But hope? Hope was a foreign concept to them.

I spent the rest of the day gently guiding them toward the understanding of hope. I challenged them to write in the notebooks I had handed out at the beginning of the seminar. "Allow God to give you a vision. Ask him to help you. Then write it down," I told them. I might as well have asked them to write *War and Peace* in Swahili. It took what seemed like forever before I saw them bend to the paper and begin writing.

One woman came to my platform and whispered that she would prefer me to talk about *sin*. She had come expecting to have a good cry as she had at the last retreat she had attended. She wanted to weep her eyes out over her shortcomings and how she had failed God. And she wanted everyone in the room to share her despair. Cupping her hand to her mouth, the woman whispered, "These women need to repent." I looked out at the sad, tired faces of the women and I thought, "It looks as if all they ever *do* is repent."

By the end of the day that sad woman was the only one who had not identified her vision. She couldn't think of a hope founded on God's love for her.

All hope comes from God.
Hope cannot be manufactured by our own efforts.
Hope isn't something we drum up by our optimism.
Hope is the blessed assurance of our future destiny based on God's love.
Only the Holy Spirit can reveal God's love, and only he can give us hope.

Don't be fooled. We tend to treat pain as an enemy. We want to avoid it. Our very first encounters with pain tell us that it is a very bad thing. "The stove is *hot!*" Mommy yelps in terror. Baby reaches for a sharp object—"No-no!" When baby trips and falls, Mommy's face pales in fear. "Did baby hurt herself?" As we grow up, we're admonished, "Look both ways or you'll get hit by a car." "Drink your milk, or you won't grow." Our first words include cute euphemisms such as "Ouchie-ow," "Ow-ie," and "hurtie." Maybe pain is waiting around every corner, ready to nab us if we make the slightest mistake.

As adults, we often continue to develop a distorted view of pain and suffering. We want to be protected from harm and hurt. We want to keep suffering outside our lives. We try to lock it out, scare it away, fight it off, sedate it, buy it off. Hope is ignored; faith set aside.

It's not so much the pain that has us foiled, it's the fear of it. When we are afraid, the choices we make are more influenced by their risk-proofing qualities than by their inherent value to our souls.

Is Romantic Love an Antidote to Pain?

Sometimes people pursue romantic love as an antidote to pain. Think about the selection of a spouse. A "Personals" ad in the newspaper could very well read:

Female wants perfect husband. Must be handsome, have good job, and fulfill all my dreams. He must not ever find fault with me or cause me any problems whatsoever. He must love me unconditionally and take care of my every need. He must not bother me with his needs or troubles. Send photo and paycheck stubs.

Any prospective spouse who doesn't measure up to our preconceived ideas of a risk-free relationship is set aside.

We pursue painlessness as a goal, and that painlessness is proof that we count for something, that God loves us and hears our prayers. The less pain we experience, the more esteemed we feel. Love is measured as an antidote to pain, even if the love comes in the form of aggression. If we are loved, pain is somehow assuaged for a time. We have a sense of self-esteem based on the affection we receive from another.

Human love is not an antidote to pain. It nurtures a false sense of self-esteem based on human affection, not on hope in God's unconditional love. When there is a fight, a break-up, a divorce or separation, we experience what we have grown to dread since our first ouchie-ows: the deep sense of being nothing. This pain tells us we are not okay, that because all is not well with us, we are nothing.

All around us are women desperately searching for romantic love as an antidote for pain. They feel that they can at least *endure*, no matter how artlessly or ignobly, if they have a romantic attachment.

I can't begin to count the unions I've seen take place between men and women who probably never should have gotten together in the first place. These people were afraid of being alone. They confused godly hope with wishful thinking. Once these couples tied the knot, they lived as if sentenced to doing penance. They were then forced to endure.

Marriages that are without an ideal, without deep, abiding love and tenderness, simply endure. These relationships—including relationships between dating couples—are what Erich Fromm called "fusion without integrity." Fusion without integrity is based on the idea that a person other than God will answer all our needs instead of the only One who can.

The word "endure" means to carry on despite hardships—to bear with tolerance. It comes from the Latin adjective *durus,* which means "hard." The Latin verb *durare* then came into play, which means "to continue in existence." So when we are enduring, we might say we are hardening ourselves in order to continue existence.

To endure is not to persevere, which means to persist or remain constant to a *purpose, idea, or task* in the face of obstacles or discouragement. It is what the saints of old experienced in the face of intense suffering and martyrdom.

Life is more than merely enduring. If we are to do more than simply endure, we must lose our fear of suffering. We must risk being alone rather than risk our soul's best. God has put within us the potential to prevail, and because we are human beings with souls, with spirits capable of compassion and sacrifice, we can behave with courage, honor, and hope.

Check Fantasy at the Door

We relish imaginative stories. Without an imagination, we lead very bland lives. I write children's books and perform children's theater, where I allow fantasy to have free rein. When, in one of my stories, Alula-Belle Button-Top Paintbrush Soft Shoe Poocheeni Magrew flies to Ice Cream Beach to brave the attack of the Pickle Necks, I am having as much fun as the children are. It's a fantasy land that brings delight to both the children and to me.

There is a big difference, however, between a children's fantasy story and our dream that some person will come along to solve all our problems. We can call it "hope," but really it's a fantasy. We're trying to avoid or ease our pain by believing a lie. It's easy to do. See if you have developed any of these false fantasies:

- If I am good God will bless me and won't allow any harm to come to me.

- If I eat all my peas I won't get sick.

- If I work hard I'll get the raise.

- If I'm kind and loving I'll always be loved.

Identifying our assumptions helps us recognize them as fantasies. They are vain hopes, not true hopes. As the author of Ecclesiastes said, "Vanity, vanity, all is vanity." Why are such pursuits of painlessness all in vain? The answer is that God never promised us painless living. Since the day sin entered the human heart, God's promise to humanity has been one of overcoming, prevailing, and mastering personal destruction. The Old Testament rings with admonitions such as "Be strong and of good courage," and the New Testament tells us, "Let not your heart be troubled." The very fact that these words are stated tells us there will be pain and sorrow. But also inherent in these admonitions is the promise of hope—the kind only God can give.

You Can Live beyond the Mundane

The woman of hope lives beyond the mundane. She rises quietly above her fear of pain and triumphs over suffering, while others, the famous and celebrated, who boast of more banners and trophies, grin away at us from the covers of magazines and from the screens of television sets. To some people, to be uncelebrated is to be a failure. For them, fame has become an antidote to the pain and fear of being insignificant.

I know performers and artists as well as preachers and religious leaders whose main objective, above their art or religious convictions, is fame. The drive for fame can be relentless. Fame tells us, "When others notice me, applaud me, love me, follow me, I am truly alive and worthy. I will endure forever." In the absence of an awareness of God's unconditional love, the elusive pursuit of honor and prestige becomes all-important. These people find their significance in the illusory promises of fame instead of putting their hope and trust in God. *True* hope and *true* trust in the *true* God lift us above the mundane.

Death-defying hope. The unnamed noblewoman described in 2 Kings 4 and 8 was a great blessing to the prophet Elisha. Her story gives us an example of faith, hospitality, love, but even more, of *hope*. She and her husband had gone beyond the ordinary expectations of hospitality by setting aside a special room for Elisha to stay in; he was told that he could call it home whenever he needed it. Elisha enjoyed his waystation in the noblewoman's house over a period of about four years.

One thing was missing in the life of the noblewoman and her husband. They had no child. One day Elisha asked how he might repay them for their kindness. Gehazi, Elisha's servant, mentioned that the woman's husband was old and they had no children. Elisha called the noblewoman and announced, "Thou shalt embrace a son."

The woman was not given to false hope. She had accepted her childless situation. Now here was Elisha telling her a miracle would take place and she would give birth to a son after all these years. She responded with, "Don't mislead me, Man of God. Don't give me false hopes."

The story is a tender one, for the woman did give birth to a baby boy. What joy filled their home! But then, tragically, when the child was about four years old, he died of a sunstroke. Now we see that the noblewoman was noble in both earthly and heavenly terms; now we see her demonstrate true hope.

Though brokenhearted, she didn't waste any time. Immediately she rushed to find the prophet Elisha with *hope* in her heart that the prophet of God could and would restore her boy to life. *She took the jump of faith.* She didn't tell anyone else that the boy was dead because she wanted to communicate with Elisha only.

What happened? Elisha responded to her summons. He went home with her and miraculously restored the boy to life, literally breathing the life back into him.

The woman had not known whether or not she would find the prophet. She had not known if he would help her. How did she know but that it might be God's will that the boy be taken from her? She had no solid knowledge or answers. She only had *hope*. She flew out of the house to find Elisha because her hope was greater than her grief. Hope mingled with faith is powerful. *Hope propelled her forward.*

The gift of God's hope propels us beyond our ordinary limits into the loving arms of God. Nestled in the security of his all-encompassing embrace, we can release our remaining fantasies and fears. A woman who asks for the gift of hope becomes a woman of confidence and courage.

GOD SPEAKS:

I am hope.

I give you more than future glory.

I am your present glory.

I do hear you;

I do answer you.

—But Lord, how do I exercise hope?

Allow My written Word,

which throbs with the power of hope,

to enter your mind and body

like fresh blood in your veins,

new life in your thoughts...

—Lord, I need a miracle!

Relax your soul

through these trials and

perceive in the far reaches

of your mind

that I give you more than miracles...

—How do I know You'll answer and heal my loved one?

When you have My mind,

My wisdom,

My knowledge,

My understanding,

you will not panic

at the threats before you.

Instead, you will jump across

despair's dark night

as if it were a smooth, cool valley

of shadows.

Remember, I am with you.

I am with your loved one.

Do not be afraid.

Caress the sister of love,

which is My gift of hope,

and bravely

take your leap to safety,

for I have heard you

and I answer.

Part Two

∞

Taking the Leap

4

The Dynamic of Courage

∞

In the "For Women Only" survey, I ask the question, "When do you feel *most* brave and courageous?" Here is a sampling of the answers I received:

I feel most brave and courageous—

- after I've attended a wonderful, exciting church service.
- when people trust me.
- when I am well-prepared for a situation.
- when I know without question that what I'm saying or doing is right.
- when I hear a really good sermon or discussion about the Bible.
- when I get enough rest.
- when I feel the presence of God fill my life.
- when I feel loved.
- when I take time to pray.
- when I'm in charge.
- when I'm around people more timid than I am.
- when I'm with my family.
- when I know I'm losing weight.

An eighty-two-year-old woman said, "I feel the most courageous when I go to bed at night." When I read those words, I
paused and thought for a moment. Of course she felt courageous
at bedtime! She was eighty-two years old! Going to bed took
courage because she knew every night when she went to bed she
might not wake up in the morning.

Another woman wrote, "I don't feel brave—ever."

Still another wrote that she felt very courageous when she was
running for political office and campaigning. "It takes a lot of
courage for me to take my fliers and knock on doors asking people
to vote for me. Why vote for me over another candidate?"

A woman said, "I feel most courageous when my husband is
not around."

Ninety-five percent of the women, however, said they felt most
courageous when they were close to the Lord. "I feel most courageous when my prayer life and time with the Lord has been
priority," said one woman. "His presence is so real at these times. I
feel there's nothing *we* can't conquer together. Also, I feel brave
and courageous when I know he's spoken to me about his specific
will and I walk in obedience to what he has shown me."

Others expressed similar feelings: "I feel most brave and courageous after I have spent time with the Lord studying and meditating and I am sure I am in his will."

"I feel most brave and courageous when I am inspired and led
by the Holy Spirit and doing God's work. My weakness is his
strength."

"I feel most brave and courageous when I am not thinking so
much about myself but about the Lord."

The survey was distributed among mostly Christian women,
so I expected the responses to include prayer and feeling close
to God. But it was also evident to me by the percentage of

discouraged responses that we often misunderstand the true meaning of courage. It so easily slips away from us.

What *is* courage? Where does it come from?

Courage is a divine, unshakable confidence that comes directly from the heart of God to our hearts. Going from "I Can't" to "I Can" is the leap into courage.

Peter's courage. The fourteenth chapter of Matthew's Gospel illustrates courage in action. After miraculously feeding five thousand people and preaching all day, Jesus told the disciples to get into their boat and go out onto the water heading toward Capernaum on the other side. The disciples set out to sea; the Master went to prayer.

Night came on and a tempestuous storm rose up. Earlier when the disciples had set out, the water of Lake Gennesaret may have been calm. (We don't think we need courage when things are calm.) But by the time the storm had become violent, the disciples were frantic with fear. Then in the midst of the tumult, they saw Jesus *walking on the water.*

We need to realize that Jesus, sovereign over all nature—and over our fears—was walking not just on the water but on the *storm* itself.

Did this give the disciples courage? Far from it. Now their terror was compounded. They thought they were seeing an apparition. Most of our lack of courage does not come from outside forces but from inside us, from lack of knowledge of God's overriding power and what we mean to him.

"It is I," said Jesus. (He hardly had to give his name. His sheep ought to have recognized his voice.) "Take courage!"

What follows is my favorite part of the story. Peter did take courage. He said, "Lord, tell me to come to you...." And then

Jesus did the same thing as when he called Lazarus from the tomb: "Come!" he called to Peter.

And Peter walked on the water. He didn't do it just for the fun of it. His goal was to get to Jesus. He was walking toward Jesus, and the storms of life were beneath his feet.

When Peter took his eyes off Jesus and looked at the wind and roaring waves, he lost courage and began to sink. It was not the violence of the wind nor the whipping of the waves that threatened his life, it was taking his eyes from Jesus, who is the author of courage. He forgot the words "Apart from me you can do nothing" (Jn 15:5b).

Fears That Sink Us

Of course, Jesus pulled Peter up out of the water just as he pulls us up when we begin to sink in our fears. The problem I see in women is that we can spend a lifetime sinking and coming up for air, sinking and coming up for air, and still never do something about the stronghold of fear over our lives. We are in desperate need of courage and don't realize it because the fear is so subtle we can even mistake it for love. Let me explain what I mean by introducing you to a modern-day woman I'll call Sylvia.

Sylvia is a housewife with a husband and three grown sons. Sylvia continues to support her grown sons financially, giving them her household money, and even travels across town each week to her twenty-six-year-old son's apartment to clean and do his laundry.

Sylvia's story brims over with examples of sacrificing her own needs for the needs of others. When her husband gives her money to spend on herself, or when she has time on her hands to explore her own heart's desires, she becomes befuddled and depressed.

Sylvia is too fearful to consider herself truly valuable. In her own mind she is only valuable if she is not being rejected. She believes she is valuable as long as she is not denied affectionate appreciation. She fears that if she were to tell her sons "no!" when they ask her for money, they might retaliate with anger and withdraw their love. If she doesn't play the role of a maid by cleaning her able-bodied, grown-up son's apartment and washing his clothes, she thinks she might be considered a bad mother. If she doesn't cater to her husband's every whim, he might find another woman.

Fear leaks into her everyday life. It immobilizes her. At the supermarket, she frets, "Should I buy this product or that one?" What if she buys the wrong product? What if the family is dissatisfied? When she dresses to go out, she falls into a quandary. "Should I wear this or that?" She's not sure which outfit will be liked most. "Is my hair okay?" She's not sure if people will approve. What should she say when she talks to people? What if she's met with ridicule?

Sylvia is agreeable and quiet. She doesn't argue, make a fuss, or stand for anything. If she were to argue or show disagreement with others' opinions, they might not like her. That would be awful! Sylvia would rather climb on a bandwagon for a cause she isn't particularly interested in, as long as it is acceptable in her circle of acquaintances.

The woman who thrives on denying herself the pleasures of life may actually appear to be a selfless, giving soul. In truth hers may be a soul stung with fear. So afraid of rejection and loss of love, this woman of fear will shower her attention on others. She will be self-effacing and ragged with self-depreciation.

What Sylvia could use is some time spent listening to herself. Her neglected soul might begin to pinch her, and she might find herself in the therapist's office crying, "I don't know what's wrong with me. I have such a nice life. Why am I so depressed?"

Imagine Sylvia as a woman of confidence. Imagine her rising up out of the tomb of fear, like a Lazarus, and stepping into real life. Imagine her celebrating the world and its wonders. Imagine her staying above the water with the threats and fears of life roiling beneath her, never pulling her under. Imagine her attention fixed on the Lord, and her heart filled with thankfulness and awe at the miracle of her life empowered by love. Imagine her touching this world with her courage.

You can identify your fears. To a degree there may be a little of Sylvia in all of us. We do enjoy being liked by others, and we like to know that people appreciate us. When they are gained with a pure heart, it is gratifying to the soul to have the respect and admiration of others. But if we are motivated by fear, we are building on a damaged foundation. Nothing earned by fear brings godly results.

Fear restrains us from obtaining God-given energy and vitality. It shrivels our potential and muddies our self-image. It seeps out of us and affects the lives of those around us. Fear is a thief and a killer. It can keep us from experiencing the fullness of joy and the exuberance of life.

"Perfect love drives out fear" (1 Jn 4:18) must become real to us. I can win over my fears if I can identify them. I need to be able to admit that my actions are often motivated by underlying fears, and pull those fears out into the light of day for examination.

I think of unwelcome fears as rats—yes, *rats!*—and I name them. "Fear of Rejection," "Fear of Disapproval," "Fear of Risk," "Fear of Failure," even "Fear of Success," "Poor Me," and "I Can't"—all are unwelcome vermin crowding into the mind and heart.

When we picture our fears as ugly, hungry rats, darting out of dark corners to torment us, we can stop defending their "right" to live in our lives.

We can become free of the rats of fear. In order to do this, it is essential to learn how these rats are born, where their nests are, and how to exterminate them.

Where Do Fears Hide?

The rats of fear begin in and nest in our *thoughts*. Our behavior is the result of what we believe to be true. Our behavior is a direct reaction to what we tell ourselves. How can we recognize the lies we have believed and told ourselves? These may include: "Things shouldn't go wrong," or "People should do what I want them to," or "If I've done something bad, I'm terrible," or "If I'm at fault for something, I am a bad person."

These sorts of beliefs make great nesting material for rats of fear, also known as the "what ifs":

- What if people don't like me?
- What if I'm not appreciated?
- What if people get angry with me?
- What if people withdraw their love from me?
- What if I get into an accident?
- What if this lump is cancer (or some other deadly disease)?
- What if we'll be lonely and unhappy when we move?
- What if this airplane crashes?
- What if I never find a good husband?

- What if no one will hire me?

- What if I have to drive on the freeway?

- What if I can't work anymore?

- What if I'm too old?

- What if I run out of money?

These "what ifs" are rats. The Lord who loves you, who invites you to "come forth," is much more powerful than any rat, any fear. Remember the truth of the Word, "Perfect love drives out fear" (1 Jn 4:18).

Listen to the truth, meditate constantly on it, and speak it out loud to yourself. The constant exposure to truth will eliminate fear. The love the Lord has for you becomes clearer to you as you soak your mind in the Word of God and listen for his voice. You will hear him say, "Come forth," to you. Like Lazarus, you will be able to emerge from the tomb of fears with the truth on your lips, proclaiming loud and clear:

- "I am strong and of good courage."

- "Perfect love casts out fear" (1 Jn 4:18).

- "I can do *all* things through Christ who gives me strength" (Phil 4:13).

- "I am not a woman of fear."

- "I choose to live for God."

- "I put aside the past and its failures. Today is a new day!"

- "I am *above* the storm, holding the hand of Jesus."

You can come forth from your tomb of death and fear. You can stand in the sunlight with the breeze carrying away the reek of the empty tomb behind you. You can see Jesus standing before you, smiling at you. How he loves you! How happy he is to see you! How little those fears seem to matter now. You have walked through the valley of the shadow of death and you are alive.

> *I have called you by name, Lazarus. I have redeemed you.*
> *I have called you by name, Sylvia [your name].*
>   *I have redeemed you.*

Can you imagine Jesus asking Lazarus after raising him from the dead, "Was it scary?"

The time spent reading the Word of God, memorizing His words, and meditating on his words are critical to your walking in the confidence you were born to possess. It's an every-day process.

Let's Get Honest

We are continually tempted to indulge in fear and allow ourselves to be sabotaged. That is why Paul said, "Don't let the world around you squeeze you into its own mold, but let God remold your minds from within, so that you may prove in practice that the plan of God for you is good" (Rom 12:2, Phillips). The world's mold is formed of fear.

We're afraid of loss. Afraid of losing control. Afraid to grow up. Afraid to make mistakes, to fail. Afraid of not being liked.

Leave all these fears behind, like grave clothes. In the Book of Colossians Paul says, "Put to death, therefore, whatever belongs to your earthly nature" (Col 3:5). We may have responded to Jesus' command, "Come forth!" when we became a believer in the first place. We may have shuffled out into the sunlight as Lazarus did, wrapped in the winding-cloths of death. Now—possibly with help from others—we, like Lazarus, can be unbound and go free. Drop that thing that pulls you down. Leave it at the door of the tomb where it belongs.

Afraid to fail. Because you may have failed at a task, a relationship, or some goal in the past does not mean you are doomed to fail forever. There are no mistakes in the kingdom of God, only lessons. Sometimes it takes us longer to learn our lessons than we'd like. Give yourself the right to fail. Fail with flair!

Don't be like a woman I'll call Jean. She is a woman who tries valiantly to do the right thing at all times. She is compulsive about being on time, paying bills when they're due, washing the car once a week, and a host of other duties and obligations. She fulfills them all faithfully. She doesn't take chances.

In the face of the storms of life, such as her husband's problems at work and his infidelities with other women, she turns her head and pretends she doesn't see what is going on. Her children are very upset with her. The family is crumbling. They protest her passive attitude. But Jean is just too afraid to face the big problems that loom on her horizon. She doesn't realize how she is punishing those around her with her lack of courage.

Afraid of not being liked. Hands down, this is the number-one feeling we can't face with courage. We say: "I don't want to go to that new group because the people are cliquey and stuck up." (In other words, "I'm afraid in a new situation. What if I don't make friends?") "I'm afraid of my new boss at work. He's moody and unpredictable." (In other words, "I don't think he likes me.")

"I'm not going to join them. Those people are pathetic losers." (In other words, "Maybe I'm a pathetic loser, too.")

We become judgmental when we're afraid and unsure of ourselves. Take Debbie, for instance. Debbie appears to be the perfect Christian. She attends church, serves on various committees in the church, and helps people who are in need whenever she can. But Debbie is judgmental and without mercy when it comes to other people's failures. She judges people by her own fearful "what if" standards, not God's. When a member of her family strays from her set of rigid ideals, she becomes impatient and unforgiving. Her fears and uncertainty have alienated her from her loved ones. She fears that if rules are not strictly obeyed, doom will result. She is afraid of her *own* failure.

If you suspect somebody is angry with you or that you've offended someone, don't draw back from those feelings. Express them. Say something like, "Have I offended you? How can I make it right?" Permit your loved ones to hear words like "Honey, are you angry with me? How can I make it right between us?"

Fear should never be ignored, stifled, denied, or lied about. We need to remind ourselves to listen to our fears as well as the fears of those around us. Our example of courage will help others be as courageous as we are. Our family and friends will learn to do the same as they follow our lead.

When we can't face the fact that our fears motivate our actions, we set ourselves up for more failure, more fears, more trouble.

Courage in Action

It takes courage to admit our fears and shortcomings. Can you imagine being brave enough to say, "Yes, I acted rudely because

I'm feeling envious of your success." Or, "I'm sorry I didn't come to your dinner party. I wasn't ill and we did find a baby-sitter. It was that I was afraid of meeting new people and maybe not making a good impression, so I stayed home."

When we are afraid to make mistakes it is usually because we have had to pay so dearly for them in the past. You feel freer to talk about your mistakes with someone who is completely accepting of you, because that person will not berate or find fault with you. When you are allowed to express your feelings without fear, you are not so tempted to talk yourself out of them before you understand them. We all need a safe, caring person who will listen to us attentively and love us in spite of our failures.

When you are afraid to admit your true feelings, you go on deceiving yourself and feeling bad. Others, then, can become targets of your frustration. Also, to those who need your courageous spirit most, you have no example to give.

When you are allowed to admit your fears openly, you find it isn't necessary to wear a false mask of self-assurance which can appear as haughtiness. Persons of high achievement often feel they can't afford to admit to the fears of inadequacy that almost everyone feels at some time or another.

You *can* move from "I Can't" to "I Can" with courage. The Bible gives us very definite guidelines for a life of confidence and strength. "Put off your old self... Be made new in the attitude of your mind(s) ... Put on the new self, created to be like God in true righteousness and holiness" (Eph 4:22-24).

You *can* change your self-talk. You *can* change your attitudes toward life and God. You *can* turn fear into courage, worry into faith, doubt into hope. You *can* change an "I'm not worth much" mentality into bold confidence. You are who God says you are.

What if you don't know who you are? What if you don't seem

to have any outstanding abilities? You may tell yourself, "I can do all things through Christ who makes me strong," but you know that reciting Scripture verses won't give you instant success, if, for example, you don't know how to drive a sixteen-wheeler or speak Persian or start a business. An "I Can" mentality is not merely a form of wishful thinking.

Recognizing your Can'ts and Cans means to evaluate your strengths and weaknesses. Let me give you an example from my own experience.

Recently I became involved in what I thought was a good business venture. At the beginning it seemed to be a good investment of time and effort and thus a wise decision on my part to be involved. I felt the endeavor was a worthy cause, and everyone stood a chance to profit.

As time went on, I realized I was sadly lacking in the skills necessary to make the venture a success for me.

"Where is my confidence, my courage?" I asked myself. I decided to listen to God. Instead of bruising my soul by churning with anxiety over the situation, I got out my Bible. In Jeremiah 29:11, I found, "I know my plans for you. They are for good and not for evil."

I came to recognize and accept that there is a level of skill and ability I *don't* have. I had to stop and learn more about what I was doing. I had to become educated and more skilled. I am happy to say the venture has become more successful than we had counted on in the beginning. I learned a great lesson through it all.

Problems arise when we think we can do something requiring skills we don't possess. There are times when it takes more courage to admit we can't do a thing than it does to struggle on trying to accomplish something we weren't meant to accomplish. It's not bad or shameful to be unskilled at something. A thing may appear easy and manageable, but once engaged in it, we discover we're way over our heads. Then suddenly we're under an avalanche of insecure feelings and self-doubt. In order to compensate for these feelings we become defensive, belligerent, unpleasant. Our courage is misdirected.

Take a careful inventory of your skills and abilities. Be honest about your shortcomings. What you will gain through an "I Can" attitude in these instances is the confidence to persevere, practice, and *learn*. The Lord will help you *learn* new skills through your courage to try. He will help you as you arduously push through the hard work of becoming educated in a chosen art, profession, or skill. You *can* move from "I Can't" to "I Can" as you earnestly give the task your best efforts. I am so happy I was courageous enough to learn about a business I could have failed miserably at.

What if you lose interest or change your mind? Or perhaps even after giving a couple of years to a task, you still don't receive the desired results? What do we do when we fail to reach our original goal? Do we sulk in a corner with feelings of inadequacy? Do we feel bitter and angry over a misguided venture? Do we consider our time and effort wasted?

No. Courage tells us there are no mistakes, only lessons. Courage tells us to multiply the good. What we learn from our experiences is what has value and importance and reinforces our courage to continue on. Our "I Can'ts" can be transformed into "I Cans." I *can* be courageous.

> Experience doesn't teach us a thing.
> It's what we DO with that experience that counts.

The Lord puts his arms around us and hides us as an eagle hides her young in the warmth of her feathers. We are hidden in him, hidden in his presence and his love. He is all love. His words are love. His actions are love.

In our hours of solitude spent with the Lord alone, through his power of love, we hear his voice across the waves of the storms of life. His voice pierces through our own inner weaknesses and fears. It is the voice that floods us with new courage. His voice is soft at first. There is no tension in that voice, no anxiety, no fear. It is a pure sound—unworldly. It is incredibly still and small, yet rises above every storm of life and every fear.

GOD SPEAKS:

Sweet child of mine,

    there is nothing to fear.

I have said to trust Me at all times,

    because I am a refuge; I am a shield;

    I am Help—there is safety and rest

in releasing your many worries to Me.

    I have told you to trust Me

and nestle, like a young bird

    beneath the shadow of its mother's

mighty wings where it is safe.

    Trust Me to be Me.

Trust removes the rumbling mist of fear.

    Let it be settled in your mind

that your life, your work, your loves

    your health, your prayers,

    your past, your future

    are constantly guarded

    by My mercy and love.

You are soldered into the center of My eye.

    Trust Me.

PSALM 62:8; 115:9-11; 32:10;
MATTHEW 6:33, 34; ISAIAH 35:4; PSALM 103:4,5;
DEUTERONOMY 32:10; ISAIAH 62:3

5

The Dynamic of Fullness

∞

The Dynamic Key of Love introduces us to the abundance of life. The Dynamic Key of Hope gives us a vision of God's will for our lives and the path to follow. The Dynamic Key of Courage gives us the power to follow his will and to remain in the center of his heart. Now we take the leap to the Dynamic of Fullness.

Being full does not mean being partially empty. It means being *full*. Fullness differs from wholeness in that when a thing is whole there are no broken pieces lying about. Fullness, on the other hand, can be achieved with a chipped or sometimes even cracked vessel.

"My cup overflows," David sings in Psalm 23. We don't know what kind of cup he refers to. Whether you have a golden goblet or an old, chipped clay mug, full is full. Whether your cup is as big as a ship or as small as a thimble, full is full. It is what goes *into* the vessel that makes it full. The Dynamic of Fullness asks only that your cup be filled—not just halfway but until it overflows.

David's cup was full to overflowing because of his relationship with the Lord, and because it was full, David was not in want. "The Lord is my shepherd, I shall not be in want," he exclaims in the famous first verse of the psalm. These words, a joyful praise unto the Lord, show us that want has primarily to do with the condition of the heart. When our souls are desperate and hungry for God, we are in want. When the love of God fills our needs, we "shall not want." Even when we walk through the valley of the shadow of death, we can be full of confidence and courage. Death is only a shadow.

David tells us in the psalm that he chooses to enjoy the goodness of the Lord all the days of his life. Because he knows the heart and mind of his shepherd intimately, he can proclaim with confidence that goodness and mercy will follow him all of his days.

He placed his needs in the hands of God and in so doing lifted his soul to a higher place than his needs. David's hours spent in solitude as a shepherd gave him much experience listening to God's voice. David's soul was full.

He did not allow his needs to hinder his trust in God. "To you, O Lord, I lift up my soul, in you I trust" (Ps 25:1). All too often we say we trust the Lord for our needs but we aren't certain what that means.

Needs of a Woman: The Basic Needs List

It is important to identify what we consider needs. Some needs are unrealistic and destructive. You may think you need to make a lot of money to be happy. In your pursuit of money, you may leave other needs in your life unsatisfied.

Needs are not demands. Some needs you have are quite basic, and it is important they be met. We all have basic and realistic needs for:

- confidence in ourselves
- friendship and a sense of belonging
- respect for ourselves and others
- trust in something and someone, including ourselves
- the ability to think and reason
- creativity in our everyday life
- freedom of choice
- self-love, which is the footing upon which love of others rests
- self-discipline, which is the pulse of living free
- mercy for ourselves and others
- nurturing and giving to others and our world
- intimacy with God.

Examine this list carefully. (Key #9, The Dynamic of the Physical Body, will further discuss how we tend to hurt our bodies when our needs are not met. We will also see how we will bless our bodies when we see to it that our needs are met.)

The source of much of our frustration and hurt is the violation of and inattention to our Basic Needs List. Earlier I mentioned the misguided need to make a lot of money as a factor that might postpone the fulfillment of other more pressing needs, such as the need for friendship and a sense of belonging.

When you are especially busy or when you are pursuing a goal that takes most of your time and energy, be sure to check the Basic Needs List. Reward yourself for your hard work by being certain, for instance, that you give your need for creativity some room in your schedule. Pay special attention to your need for intimacy with God. Don't ignore your needs or push them aside.

When you realize your first and primary need is to consciously live in oneness with God, the other needs fall into place. Your soul needs its quietness with God in order to be filled with him. Fullness begins with the Dynamic of Love and the Dynamic of Solitude. It is a sad effort to seek fullness and self-worth outside of God's love.

The Lord Jesus will show you his heart in your solitude. He will guide you, open up his will for you, and free you from the frustrating labor of approval-seeking. God already has given you his stamp of approval. You don't have to earn it. He wants your life to be full of the knowledge of his love.

We create our own world when we know who we are. Identified with Christ, we're elevated from the miseries of allowing life to just fall on us in whatever manner it chooses. We stop allowing other people to make our decisions for us because we have confidence in God's loving presence in our souls. We can now listen to the needs of our souls.

What If You Ignore Your Needs?

The Dynamic of Fullness requires courage. Maribelle sits across from me explaining her resolve to leave a relationship of five years. She has remained in the relationship in spite of not being in love because it was more comfortable to stay than to break it off. She wants to start dating other men. Her voice wobbles, tears fall. "It's so haaard," she weeps, "but I'm thirty-five years old. I want to get married and have babies. That won't happen with Eddy."

"It's taking courage on your part to break up the relationship, isn't it?" I ask.

"I suppose so, but ..."

"It would be easier for you to remain in the relationship like you've been doing for the past five years and not make waves, wouldn't it?"

"Sure—I've tried a bunch of times to break it off, but I always go back."

"But this time you're choosing to take the hard way by breaking up a relationship that you know isn't right for you. I think that's courageous."

"Are you saying I've got courage?"

"Yes," I tell her.

But Maribelle isn't convinced. She's worried. She hasn't thought about evaluating her basic needs.

"Eddy is so vindictive!" she continues. "I never know what he'll say or do. I'm afraid he's going to trash me to all his friends. People will think I'm the reason for the breakup. They'll think I'm a terrible person."

She explained her many attempts to break the tie with Eddy in the past, but each time she tried, she was manipulated back into the relationship. Not only did she have a biting fear of her boyfriend's retaliation, but she was frightened of being alone and, as she put it, "on the market again."

Maribelle's attitude toward herself was that she was a weak and unlovable person. With this attitude, she sought those situations and relationships that *proved* what she basically believed about herself. She allowed others to direct her life for her, including her boyfriend. Even in the breakup, he controlled the situation. Not breaking up had been easier for her than facing the consequences of a breakup, even though the relationship was a destructive one.

It took time to show Maribelle that she had enough courage within her to face the consequences of the breakup.

I listened carefully to Maribelle, watching for the trigger words that would show me what was truly going on in her life. I could hear that she gave herself messages she was not paying any attention to. Since she was not listening to herself, I knew she was a long way from knowing herself. She was a long way from the Dynamic of Fullness.

It was crucial for Maribelle to learn that she was 100-percent lovable to God. She had to lift the cup of her life to God to fill.

There is a happy ending to Maribelle's story. She decided to change her thinking. She not only went for private weekly counseling, she began attending regular Bible studies and church. She left Eddy and didn't date anyone else until she felt her footing in the Lord was solid enough to be able to follow his will in her choices and actions. She learned to embrace solitude and listen for God's voice through the Word of God. She told me she carried her Basic Needs List in her purse, and in her prayer time went over them with the Lord in order to understand more fully how precious her life was to him. Two years have gone by, and she is now not only serving on the board of the women's Ministry Department of her church, she is helping other women realize the Dynamic of Fullness in their lives.

Often we don't know what is good for us, we don't know what we want or need, and we allow others to make our decisions for us. When women choose situations because someone else made the choice for them first, tremendous unhappiness can result. A good motto to have is "Life doesn't happen to me, I happen to life."

We must learn and recognize our needs before we can have them fulfilled in our lives. One of those needs is to have mercy on ourselves when the "shadow side" of our personality surfaces.

Good, bad, or otherwise—God loves you. The Dynamic of Love gives us permission to look at the shadow side of ourselves, as well as the bright side, and treat both with respect.

Your shadow side is the side you are not proud of, the side you don't particularly want others to see, the side that bruises your soul and the souls of others. It is the side that sabotages your hopes and dreams and makes decisions without God's wisdom. The shadow side must not be ignored or denied. Pay attention to it. When you are unpleasant, when you display fits of anger, when you lie or cheat or sink into a morass of depression, that's your shadow side.

The traditional Christian teaching I've heard most of my life told me to banish everything negative, get rid of it, ignore it, deny it. Do what you must, but cut it out *now!* People who use this approach want to get the process over with; they want immediate relief from all negativity. They may seek prayer and deliverance; often, however, prayer and deliverance are only the beginning of a process that brings godliness, wisdom, and true deliverance. Without seeing the core of what hurts us, we simply come up with explanations for our unpleasant behaviors and actions that don't take our basic needs into account. If we fail to figure out what's wrong or missing, we chalk it all up to "sin" and let it go.

Jesus did not say he loves only the good parts of you—he loves *all* of you! Realize that ALL of you is loved and valued, and is important. You must listen to your shadow side before you can deal with it. We must realize that we do not always behave as we ought to because of unmet needs. When we have mercy on ourselves, we begin to see where the leaks in the cup of our souls are. We may not find a quick fix, but turning from the shadows to the light of deliverance is a process that begins by having mercy on ourselves. It takes mercy and courage to admit where we are weakest.

Kay was a young woman who didn't listen to or try to understand her shadow side. She saw everything in life as black or white. Things were either all or nothing. Good versus bad. Right versus wrong.

Early in her life Kay had decided that she was going to be a surgeon when she grew up. Her decision was largely due to the influence of her parents. Her father was a medical doctor and her mother was a psychiatrist. Kay worked hard all her life to please her parents. For the most part, she had succeeded. They were justifiably proud of her when she got into the premed program at a prestigious university, and they were certain her future looked promising.

But Kay couldn't seem to keep her grades up. Eventually it became evident that she simply did not have the ability to pursue such an academically challenging program. To the enormous dismay of her parents, she left the university.

When Kay quit school it was as though she had quit life. She withdrew from her friends and closed herself off from family. She stopped going to church. She began experimenting with drugs, spending days and weeks on end watching TV and consuming nothing more than candy bars and black coffee.

Because she had lost a goal she had identified with so strongly, Kay considered herself less than nothing. She did not hear her heart's cry—"I want something I haven't found yet." She did not consider turning her time of heartbreak into a time of self-discovery. Instead, she retreated from the world around her. She saw only the past. For Kay, there was no future.

The disappointment she had caused her parents gnawed at her. She couldn't face them, couldn't bear to see their expressions or listen to the admonitions she feared they would regale her with. Oddly enough, her parents claimed later they would have been proud of their daughter no matter what profession she chose. They just wanted her to be "happy."

Perhaps Kay would have been happy as a botanist, astronomer, lifeguard, or poet, but she didn't give herself the opportunity to discover the niche her life was created for. Six months after dropping out of school Kay committed suicide.

Kay's feeling of failure and loss of self was more than she could stand. Her life had been led by the fantasy that becoming a surgeon would make her parents proud of her. Without her dream, she felt she had no right to exist. Kay's example shows us how strongly our beliefs affect our behavior. Her shadow side took over. She developed a habit of despair. She saw only right/wrong, succeed/fail. And it grew so out of proportion, she then saw fail/die.

Sacrificing Your Wants

There are times when we may choose to set aside our wants for the good of another. Love makes us willing to sacrifice our wants for another's sake. It is a natural part of the prospering of the soul to give and to sacrifice for another's good.

Wants are not Basic Needs. However, if you will look again at the Basic Needs List, these needs are not ones you can relinquish—ever. You can give up a desire to go to the beach instead of the mountains or to eat Chinese food instead of Italian, but you can't give up the confidence you need in order to live your life. You can exchange tennis for bowling, but you can't exchange self-respect or mercy for *anything*.

Many women feel they need to drop *all* their wants for another. This is just as off-kilter as ignoring their needs, and a lot of unhappiness will result. When we drop our wants, goals, dreams, and preferences for the wants of another, living solely for his or her supposed happiness, we are doing damage to our souls. By the same token, nobody should be expected to set aside his or her goals, dreams, and preferences for the sake of our wants, living solely for our supposed happiness.

The Woman as Little Girl

The little girl sees the world through her wants. The child says, "I'm hungry," and it doesn't matter what the circumstances around her are, she thinks only of her own condition of hunger. Children throw tantrums when they can't have their own way because to a child, nobody else's needs or wants count as much as their own. The child has no way of knowing the world doesn't exist just for him or her. It isn't that the child is bad; that behavior and attitude is quite appropriate for a child.

Unfortunately, many women still live within the parameters of a child's mind, and they refuse to live in the Dynamic of Fullness. It's a convenient and familiar "I Can't" role for a woman to play. Many women simply won't grow up. It isn't that they can't grow up, it's that they *won't*. These women expect the world to take care of them. They expect a big, strong man to handle the tasks they think are too difficult for them to manage. They look for a man to support them and earn the money. Little Girl Women even call their husbands "daddy."

The Little Girl Woman is led by her emotions. She is afraid of danger. She is more helpless than a child because a child can learn and grow. The Little Girl Woman thinks it's feminine to refuse to grow up.

It is a tragic thing to see a thirty-five-year-old woman who is still a child. Sometimes women in their fifties and sixties go on thinking and behaving like little girls. They're afraid of the big bad world. Their primary characteristic is their need to be taken care of.

The Little Girl Woman can't stand it if other females are prettier, get more attention, or own more possessions than she does. She hates it if another female gets ahead of her or is more accomplished. She snubs females she is jealous of. She gossips, tells lies, and purposely tries to hurt other women who, in her little girl mind, are just nasty playmates.

The Little Girl Woman gets her way with men by being helpless and coy. She is convinced that her "I Can't" way of doing things is adorable to men. She whines and fusses when she doesn't get her way and believes men should be big and strong so she can remain little and weak.

Little Girl Wife. The Little Girl Wife doesn't make her own decisions. She asks her husband for permission to do things the way a child asks her parents. She tries to be a "good girl," but most of the time she is extremely selfish and wants her own way. She compares her life to the lives of other married women and is depressed if she doesn't have what they have.

Little Girl Businesswoman. The Little Girl Businesswoman gets upset easily and may even cry at her desk when things go wrong. She pouts and frets and hopes someone will come along to make the bad go away. When problems arise, she blames others and complains bitterly about the horrible stress she's under.

Little Girl Friend and Lover. The Little Girl Friend and Lover has temper tantrums. She stamps her foot and juts out her chin, and resorts to tears or silence when things don't go her way. She can't stand an argument she doesn't win. She believes loved ones should agree with her and give in to her desires.

Little Girl Mother. The Little Girl Mother has a difficult time with real children because they steal attention from her and force her to be selfless. She likes to play with her dollies (her children), but as they get older the Little Girl Mother can't allow them to develop as individuals. She wants to control them and make them like herself. When her children don't do what she wants, the Little Girl Mother thinks she has the right to be angry and offended. If they don't obey her wishes, she thinks they are rebellious and terrible.

Little Girl Christian. The Little Girl Christian is always confused about the will of God. She can't figure out why God doesn't remove all the evil in the world. She thinks God should stamp out all hunger, war, disease, and pestilence from the world because, after all, he's *God* and he can do *anything*.

The Little Girl Christian can't seem to move deeper in her spiritual life. She especially doesn't like the idea of the Dynamic of Solitude. To be alone is like punishment to her. To the Little Girl Christian, the Dynamic of Hope is just another term for wishful thinking. She *likes* wish lists! The Little Girl Christian thinks the Dynamic of Courage is for people much stronger than she is because, after all, she is essentially helpless and little. The Little Girl Christian doesn't like to wait. She wants her prayers answered right away. She wants what she wants *now*.

When we were little girls, we talked, thought, and reasoned like little girls. But now we are grown-up women and it's time to put childish ways behind us. It's time to grow up. It's time for us to be brave and do hard things. It's time to tell ourselves, "I will not live my life as a dependent child. I will take my place in the kingdom of God as a woman of confidence. I will put away my childish ways.

When I was a child, I talked like a child, I thought like a child, I reasoned like a child. When I became a [woman] I put childish ways behind me.   1 CORINTHIANS 13:11

God Helps You Know Yourself

We *can* shatter the defeating habits that have held us bound in childishness. We *can* change. The Dynamic of Fullness requires us to empty our cups of the past habits of behaving as Little Girl Women. We must realize that avoiding pain and trouble is childish; we must grow up.

You see, the Lord *knows* our true needs, because he *formed* them. They are important to him. He wants you to think *his thoughts* in order to allow the Dynamic of Fullness to happen in your life.

Observe your dependent behavior and ask yourself what it means. Is it reasonable? Or are you so dependent on others that it is interrupting the flow of God's fullness in your life? It's important to get at the root of these self-sabotaging behaviors. Besides the "little girl" behaviors I have already described, some of us are too busy being *victims* or living dependent lives to break free into God's fullness. We feel helpless.

Dependence Needs That Make Us Feel Helpless

Helplessness is:

- Seeing situations as impossible and finding no way out. If you stay helpless and trapped by life and its discouragements, you'll bask in bad feelings and keep yourself isolated from genuine closeness to others, and you will diminish your own potential for greatness. You'll go about frowning and complaining and never have to reach inside yourself to that place you fear is empty.

- Believing the lie that any effort on your part to go from "I Can't" to "I Can" will only result in failure or rejection. This belief is largely due to an underlying feeling of worthlessness. "Everything happens to me" is a frequent exclamation that reinforces our feelings of worthlessness.

- Thinking outside circumstances are just too overwhelming to handle. These can be the sickness of a loved one, wayward children, obnoxious employers or employees, or any circumstance outside your control. The truth is, circumstances *can* be handled. But what really bothers us is that we cannot rigidly *control* things. Our misbeliefs may include "It's terrible when bad things happen to me"; "It's terrible when I can't control the outcome of events"; "It's terrible that I have to be in a difficult and painful situation."

The lies we tell ourselves need to be replaced with the truth. Though we can't control the world, we can be at peace knowing we are in the care of a God who hears our every concern and prayer.

The meaning we attach to circumstances affects our reasoning.

Take, for example, the woman who forbids herself to be truly happy. "I can't handle this situation," she may say, not, "I can do something positive to enhance the situation." "I can't handle this relationship," she may complain, not, "I can do something positive and assertive to enrich this relationship." When she says, "I can't change this situation into something agreeable," she really means, "I won't give any effort to make things better, period." I call that being a "tragedienne." You are sabotaging yourself if you've made yourself so helpless.

The tragedienne becomes so detached from herself that she stops feeling she is the actual person living her life. This is something that has been defined as schizoid alienation, and it happens so often that it has become a sign of our times. Uncertainty about life itself and our very existence is at the core of much neurotic behavior. We become naïve to the godly values we crave that will help us to feel good about ourselves and our relationship to God.

A common scenario for the tragedienne is an exaggerated dependence upon others to provide her happiness. In this regard, she is not much different from the Little Girl Woman.

We *make* ourselves victims by our thinking. If we believe our happiness lies in the lap of fate, other persons, or even in what we consider favorable circumstances, we are entertaining victim thinking. As victims we are always in a state of longing. Nothing seems satisfying or gratifying. Victims, or tragediennes, don't really cherish other people because they so desperately *need* them. They often regards loved ones as commodities.

No other person can fill God's place in our souls. It is through him that our souls find the fulfillment we crave. The Lord gives us a unique and perfect awareness of our value to him and the world—no other person can do that. His love keeps us from falling and saves us from defeat, deceit, and danger. He helps us examine the roots of our thinking, shows us where we're sabotaging our-selves, gives us power to help us change.

Remove from your thinking the false idea that you have to prove something to God before he will move in your life. That idea says, "Our mirror image is what counts most." God is inter-ested in your *soul*, your real self.

Before Jesus raised Lazarus from the dead, he didn't ask, "Was he a good boy?" When Jesus called to Peter, "Come!" across the stormy waves, he didn't preface it with, "First tell me what you've done for me today." When God calls us to himself, he doesn't do a credit check first.

Gomer, a biblical tragedienne. Gomer was a sad figure of a woman led by her lusts. She left her husband Hosea at home and went off with other men, chasing empty and vain gratification. Hosea was a good man, a prophet who loved God, who had mar-ried Gomer out of obedience to God. But Gomer was easily beguiled and must have told herself there was something better out there.

Gomer ran away with another man, only to become one of his household slaves. We could call Gomer's story "The Woman Who Refused to Love Herself or God." When we love ourselves as God loves us we don't chase false promises, gods of evil, and acts of shame. Gomer was to be an imprisoned slave for the rest of her life, but Hosea came to her rescue after God spoke to him. Hosea's love was great enough to forgive her faithlessness and betrayal, just as God's love for us is great enough to keep us from the tragedi-enne's fate. The Lord is drawing you into the folds of his loving-kindness. You aren't required to pass an exam at the end of the term before being allowed into the graduating class of the saints.

As you listen to the Lord speak to you, become aware of the wonderful safety in his love and acceptance.

As the Father has loved me, so have I loved you. Now remain in my love.   JOHN 15:9

Despairing and fearful words are not in the Lord's vocabulary. They must leave yours, too.

In the place of solitude we listen to hear God's voice, and he calls us out of victim-dependency needs. God inhabits our solitude—our place of confidence and strength. We are no longer tragediennes. We are women of confidence. The Dynamic of Fullness is ours. He wants our cup full and overflowing. In the fullness he speaks.

GOD SPEAKS:

If you see yourself alone,

      your heart quaking—I see you.

If your eyes dull, your soul despairs,

      I am with you. I am a giving God

and I love you.

I am telling you to conquer

      impossible worlds.

wield the powerful sword of the Spirit

      and the mighty banner of faith

that I give to you.

      Fly the heights and scour the depths,

freely move through clouds,

      soar across the earth with arms outspread,

open to life and love and productivity.

      Celebrate the rising of the sun

and the going down of the same!

      Greet the dawn with trembling expectation!

I am there.

      I am a giving God and I love you.

I am there in sunlight and in shadows.

I am there in hunger and in fatness,

in your youth and in old age.

      I stick to you like your own skin.

The mountains of the earth will shake

      and crumble,

but My tender love for you is never shaken—

      not a shiver,

not a breath,

      not the barest vibration or change,

I am a giving God and I love you.

6

The Dynamic of Confidence

❧

In this chapter, we are going to see how the Dynamic of Confidence affects not only our lives but the lives of those around us. We will examine how history plays a role in the confidence of the modern woman of today. We will see the importance of the Dynamic of Confidence in our relationships with others. And lastly, we will learn more about the spirit of control and how it affects our confidence.

What does true confidence look like? Let's look again at Matthew 14 and the experience of Peter when he walked across the stormy waves of the sea toward Jesus. You remember that Peter stepped out of the boat onto the water after Jesus told him, "Come." Peter did well until he took his eyes from Jesus and looked at the wind and the raging sea. Then he began to sink. He called out in desperation, "Lord, save me!"

Peter was out in the middle of the sea about to drown, and to whom did he cry out for help? Not to the men in the boat but to Jesus, who was also in the middle of the raging water. Peter knew the men in the boat couldn't help him. It took the One who could stand on top of the storms of life to rescue him from death.

Instantly, Jesus reached out his hand and caught Peter.

In that silent act, that divine rescue, we see a beautiful example of the Dynamic Key of Confidence. Peter is in the middle of the sea at four in the morning, while a horrific storm is sending giant waves crashing all around him. He clings to Jesus, who holds him tightly. No boat. No life raft. No life preserver. Jesus just stands on top of the storm holding Peter in his arms. What a picture!

"You of little faith," Jesus said to Peter. "Why did you doubt?" A few minutes later when they climbed into the boat, the wind died down and the storm passed. But the dynamic moment of confidence had already taken place out in the middle of the sea, at the height of the storm when Peter threw himself into Jesus' arms.

How confident would you feel being rescued from drowning by someone standing on the water without so much as a life preserver on? When you allow the Holy Spirit to permeate your mind and soul, you realize Jesus is who he says he is, and all of your confidence springs from this knowledge. You don't need proof or reason for his power. You need him. He is the source of the Dynamic of Confidence.

I've asked myself many times why women seem to be less confident than men. Why is it that we have a difficult time grasping the Dynamic of Confidence? To understand ourselves better, let's look back in history to see how women have fared.

Women throughout history have struggled with the issue of identity. Though Jesus never sanctioned prejudice based on sex, class, or race, women have been subjected to inferior positions since ancient times.

The Church. In earlier times the only way a woman could serve the Lord with all her gifts was to join an order of nuns. Between A.D. 100 and A.D. 500 women were drawn to the ascetic life of contemplation and prayer because life in the convent offered a woman freedom to worship the Lord and find her identity in her relationship to him. Her only other option in life was to marry and have children, often with a man not of her own choosing. It was in the church that women found the most enduring and powerful roles. The vocation of the saint provided a louder voice and broader outreach than did any secular woman's role.

During the years A.D. 600-700 countless heroic women kept Christianity alive by offering up their bodies in martyrdom rather than deny their faith in Jesus Christ. The Reformation drove women from the cloistered life, and with the dissolution of the nunneries, women lost their last chance of spiritual service outside the narrow confines of husband, home, and children.

Martin Luther's views on the inferiority of women are no secret. The Reformers as a whole held that women existed for the comfort and well-being of men. Calvin, for instance, explained to friends what he wanted in a woman: "A woman who is gentle, pure, modest, economical, patient, and who is likely to interest herself about my health."*

Today in this country we women aren't flogged and murdered by the ruling class for teaching the Word of God. We aren't tortured and burned at the stake for proclaiming our faith in Christ. But still we feel inferior and we battle for confidence.

The World We Live in Today

So many factors figure into our lack of confidence in today's world. What Jesus taught and accomplished during his earthly ministry stands in obvious contrast to what is proclaimed even today. Religious leaders have led women to believe we are inferior

---

*"Quoted in Edith Dean, *Great Women of the Christian Faith* (New York: Harper & Row, 1959), 322.

people. In the name of "spiritual authority" or "divine order," women have sometimes been subjected to playing roles that have denied their spiritual gifts.

The good news is that when we stand before Christ, he sees us not as male or female but as individuals. The Bible tells us to obey God and his Word. "For there is one God and one mediator between God and men [and women], the man Christ Jesus" (1 Tm 2:5).

As individuals we are each to be in submission to the lordship of Christ (see Ephesians 5:22). Jesus Christ is to be a woman's first love. When he is not, the woman becomes prone to worshiping other gods—her husband, her children, and her home.

It is important to note that in Ephesians 5:25-30 Paul calls on a husband to love his wife to the point of being willing to die for her. To love her "as Christ loved the church" means to sacrifice everything for her. Submission in love is not a one-sided act. Divine love shapes the godly relationship between a man and a woman and creates a truly blessed marriage.

The modern-day church has done much to help women become more confident, whole people, but we still have a long way to go. Many churches in the United States still treat single women, including the divorced and widowed, as spiritually handicapped; and women in general are still looked upon as subordinates. I'm not here to solve the problems of oppression and patriarchy, but to help open our eyes to some of the contributing factors to women's lack of confidence and feelings of inferiority.

Many of us have been told since we were little girls that it's better to be pretty than brave, or that girls should be quiet and not intrusive, or that boys are supposed to be strong and girls are supposed to be weak. Some girls are told they are tomboys simply because they are energetic and inquisitive. Because a girl likes to wear jeans and play with trucks, she may be labeled unfeminine. One woman I know was taught that she shouldn't spend too much time reading because boys don't like girls who are too intelligent and accomplished.

A very talented and accomplished musician friend of mine was told as a child that if she didn't stop playing the piano she'd never get a boyfriend. This same woman, who now thrills millions with her music, recently told me that after one of her concerts in our city, a young lady said to her, "I'll bet men are really intimidated by a female as brilliant and talented as you are, right?"

How are we supposed to feel good about ourselves if who we are is somehow "intimidating"? How are we supposed to have confidence if the world around us tells us who we are is not acceptable? The message my friend received was that she was not being what she was supposed to be, unintimidating, or I suppose "unbrilliant" is more like it.

Just recently I received a call from a man giving me advice on buying real estate. "Now remember, Marie, try not to think like a woman!" he said. I asked him what, in his opinion, did a woman think like?

"Oh, you know. Women don't think with their heads. They think with their emotions. They aren't tough enough. Women need to think more like men!"

It reminded me of some advice I was given a few years back about hiring employees for a counseling center. Two of my male advisors said, "Always remember, Marie, hire *women* for the most laborious tasks because women will work twice as hard and twice as long for half the money. You can get a woman to do the work of two or three people. A woman will work overtime and come in on weekends for no pay. You'll never find a *man* who will do that." Sadly, I knew they were right. Is it any wonder we women have a problem with confidence?

I know a female executive of a huge corporation who is the only woman in the corporation to ever hold such high office. She is probably the single most valuable employee in her company next to the president and CEO. Twice a year the company holds a weekend retreat for all the top executives. My friend has never been invited, although almost all the men are her subordinates.

When I questioned her about this inequity, she told me, "The retreats are lavish guy-thing affairs, and having a woman around would spoil things for them." So although she may hold a better job than her male counterparts, she is punished for being a female by being left out of the biggest company perk of the year.

I have worked with women for several years through the books, newspaper columns, magazine articles, and letters I have written, as well as counseling, teaching in the classroom, and public speaking. I've traveled to many countries and felt the heartbeat of many cultures, and through these experiences I've learned that though the faces and names of women may change, the problems remain similar. Even with the great strides that have been made to achieve for women equal pay for equal work, equal opportunity, spousal support of children, and other major advances for our betterment, many women remain victims of controlling situations and systems. We accept defeat and then wonder why we haven't the confidence to make the world a better place.

Once we understand the messages the world has given and continues to give us and what our history has been as women, we can measure what God tells us through his Word about women and their value. We can see ourselves in the light of tender love and high honor, and we can come out of our tombs as did Lazarus, and into the sunshine of forgiveness, understanding, mercy, and productivity.

The Proverbs 31 woman. In the tenth century B.C. women had no rights of their own and were considered of little value outside of their childbearing and housekeeping abilities. Yet the Bible speaks of the Proverbs 31 woman as having a "noble character." Her worth, says the Bible, was valued at more than rubies. She was a wife, mother, businesswoman, artist, philanthropist, and philosopher. Her confidence and integrity affected everyone who knew her. Her confidence gave her husband, her children, and her servants all the confidence they needed.

The Proverbs 31 woman demonstrates the Dynamic of Fullness as well as the Dynamic of Courage and the Dynamic of Confidence. She was not afraid. She worked vigorously. She was physically strong. She was a woman who helped others if they needed help. She didn't worry about money; instead she went out and earned it. She gave to the poor. She made sure her husband was respected. She was smart and thoughtful and had a sense of humor. She was aware that her charm and beauty would one day fade, but her integrity would survive all.

Deborah. Look at Deborah in the Book of Judges, our Jewish Joan of Arc, so to speak. She heard from God and she went to war, accomplishing the work of a man. Prophetess, ruler, warrior, poetess, and mother of Israel, she made no apologies for her position. She didn't worry about earning the acceptance of others. She didn't fret over what step to take next. She was confident. She heard from God. She told Barak to go to war against the armies of Sisera. Barak said, "I'll go if you go."

Deborah went to battle against Sisera. She fought his mighty armies and won. The victory was astounding. Here is an important key—Deborah was confident of winning *before* she went into battle. She had long-term faith in God. She trusted his Word with a deep understanding of his love and faithfulness. Instead of being burned at the stake as Joan of Arc was several centuries later, Deborah composed a love poem to God singing praises of his triumph. "I will sing to the Lord, I will sing!"

Jael. There's another heroine in this story—a wonderful woman named Jael. She was married to a man named Heber, a Kenite, who was a metalworker. Their home was a tent, and in those days everything connected with the tent was the woman's job. Jael was an expert with tent pin and maul. Sisera, the treacherous leader of the dreaded Canaanites, escaped the battle where Deborah had triumphed and happened upon the tent of Jael. It was a fatal error on the part of Sisera. He must have considered Jael a helpless, naïve thing without much spine, for after drinking milk, he fell asleep on her floor. Jael covered him and told him not to be afraid.

Imagine the ferocious leader of a nation who had cruelly oppressed your people lying asleep on your floor. Jael moved silently toward him and plunged a tent nail through Sisera's head, pinning him to the ground. The Bible tells the story with simplicity, and concludes with the words, "...and so he died." Deborah extolled Jael in her famous song of victory:

> *Most blessed be Jael,*
> *the wife of Heber the Kenite,*
> *most blessed of tent-dwelling women.*   JUDGES 5:24

Deborah knew fearlessness is the way of God. I like to think her prayer was for you and me—women of the twenty-first century—when she prayed:

> *May they*
> *who love you*
> *be like the sun*
> *when it rises in strength.*   JUDGES 5:31

Where are the Deborahs of today? Where are our Proverbs 31 women? Where are our Jaels?

Are You Building on a Solid Foundation?

Women need a solid foundation upon which to build confidence. The Ten Keys to a confident and dynamic life require a foundation centered in Christ and his Word. A dictionary definition of confidence is "a firm belief; trust; reliance." Upon *what* do we firmly believe? *What* or *whom* do we trust and rely on? If you answer, "I believe in *me*," as one woman hotly told me, chances are your confidence is shaky, weakened by delusion.

Such a woman will say to me, "I don't trust anybody except myself." But if I only trust myself, what happens when I disappoint myself, when I fall short of my own expectations? Where does my confidence go when I no longer trust myself?

A woman told me, "I'm *me*, and if people don't like it that's just too bad! I've got to be *me!*" Another said her motto was "Get on my train or get off my track." You can hear anger and frustration in those words. Certainly, *anger is not confidence; it's a reaction to a lack of confidence.*

The urge to control. There is another aspect of confidence to examine as we cover the Key of Dynamic Confidence. It is how confidence affects our relationships. It is not possible to enjoy a truly loving and healthy relationship if confidence is blatantly lacking in one or the other partner.

Let me illustrate what I mean by introducing you to Linda and Ron, who were engaged to be married. Ron was an engineer with a degree from M.I.T. Linda was an English major graduating soon from the University of Massachusetts. Their plans were to be married after her graduation and then to make their home in Vermont where Ron had an excellent job opportunity. They seemed like a compatible and happy couple, but as the wedding date approached, Ron worried that maybe he was making a mistake.

What were his concerns? "It's just that we argue so much," Ron answered. "I'm worried about it because it seems as though every time we're together we fight."

Ron insisted that he loved Linda, but began to have serious doubts about whether the decision to marry was a good one. After we talked for awhile, Ron made a discovery about himself. Ron realized that he was approaching marriage and romance in much the same way that he worked with blueprints. That is, he expected to design and control things as though he were creating plans for a piece of machinery.

Ron expected Linda to do things the way he wanted, to be the way he wanted her to be, and to make no problems for him. He expected her to be there when he wanted her to be, and if she didn't always perform smoothly and predictably, he was upset. Arguments followed, and Ron couldn't understand why.

On the other hand, Linda expected Ron to meet her every demand. She found it intolerable that he didn't do what she wanted him to do. She was unhappy that he didn't adore her for every little favor she did for him. They were a Little Boy and Little Girl Engaged Couple. It was a disastrous situation.

Relationships are often conflicts of power: Who is going to control whom? Some drastic misconceptions of love are:

- "If you say you love me, you'll let me control you without putting up an argument."
- "If you love me, you'll never hurt or disappoint me."
- "If you really love me, you'll let me dominate you."
- "If you really love me, you'll put aside your own wants and goals for mine."

When such demands are not met, the unhappy conclusion is to say good-bye to the relationship and start all over with someone else. In this way we continually set ourselves up to hurt and be hurt. This way of thinking directly opposes the Dynamic of Love we discussed in chapter one.

Why We Want to Control Others

The fear of being hurt and our lack of confidence often cause us to want to *control* our relationships with others. Intense difficulties arise because most people don't like being controlled. If they do, they need as much help as the one doing the controlling.

Linda and Ron realized their urge to control as well as their mutual lack of confidence. They decided to postpone their marriage for a year. In that time they would work hard to accept themselves as individuals and to give each other the right to love without demands and contingencies. Their relationship now has a chance of blossoming.

Married persons may believe, "Since you're married to me, you owe it to me to make my needs more important to you than your own."

A son or daughter insists, "You're my parent. You're supposed to sacrifice everything for me."

These demands, often unspoken, placed upon others, can result in frustration and conflict, and will often precede such words as "You don't care about me. You don't love me."

What you really need is to come out of the place called "the urge to control." It is a place of darkness and sorrow. Jesus and the liberating power of his love can free you to be the loving, giving person you were meant to be. The first step is to admit the urge to control.

The urge to control belongs on the floor of the cave with your other deadly urges. Jesus is calling you out of the cave of darkness into the light, where you can love and be loved.

Can you imagine Lazarus putting up a fuss when he was raised from the dead? Can you hear his protests from inside the cave as he staggers to his feet? "This isn't the way I want things to go at all! These linen wrappings are too tight, and the rock at the door is the wrong color. I want things my way! I want to control things!"

When the loving voice of God reaches your heart, especially in your time of solitude, as we discussed in Key # 2, you follow and obey without a struggle. You *can* drop your urge to control.

When the Dynamic of Love and the Dynamic of Confidence rule your emotions and thoughts, you *can* give others the right to live and love. The urge to control is an "I Can't" way of life.

Love Is a Risk That Confidence Takes

Love always includes risk. When you love somebody, you become vulnerable. The love and respect you have gained for yourself by carefully working on your Basic Needs List on page 84 is neither vain nor pride-filled. The Dynamic of Confidence gives you power to love without demanding control of the loved one or the situations you encounter. You recognize God's perfect design and purpose for you. You see your intrinsic value to him and the cherished position you hold in his heart.

The Dynamic of Confidence teaches you not only to accept yourself but to accept others. This does not mean that you go around with blind eyes refusing to admit to the problems you see in others that ultimately affect you; however, by accepting yourself and dropping unrealistic demands on yourself, you find that you are far more tolerant, loving, and understanding when it comes to others. Your confidence is centered in the love of God for you and the world.

Religious control. The urge to control can do greater harm when it is on a larger scale. For instance, a legalistic religious system can produce lifelong anguish.

A couple who came to me for counseling told me about the church they had belonged to as kids—the church they thought they loved. When they were eighteen years old they became engaged, but she became pregnant before the wedding. They were both hauled before the church board. As punishment, they were forbidden to speak to one another for one year. Not only that, they were both ostracized for one year from any fellowship with other believers in the church, and yet they were expected to attend Sunday services.

Sunday after Sunday this young man and woman sat alone in church, alienated, humiliated, and shamed. You would think the parents of the young couple would have been grieved at such cruel treatment, but they were not. They felt righteously gratified with the punishment. The young woman carried her child without support from friends, family, husband, or any other living soul. No one prayed with her, encouraged her, or rejoiced with her at the new birth.

When the year was up, the church expected the couple to re-enter the fellowship and ask forgiveness so all would be as before. However, the couple, traumatized, took their little baby and fled to another city, where they were married. You may wonder why they didn't leave the church earlier. Their answer: "We believed we had sinned, and we accepted the punishment. We wanted to be right with God again." They had not learned to have confidence in the Lord's love for them as individuals. They thought of God's will and the rules of their church as one.

This lovely couple and wonderful child were so damaged by the ignorant cruelty of so-called Christians that they spent years recovering. Fifteen years after their marriage, they sat in my counseling office seeking help for their deep-seated problems related to guilt. They had to invest much time in restructuring their thinking. Their original guilt had been compounded with interest over the years. As adults they were responsible for the way they thought about the events of their past. Now they were responsible to come to a new awareness of God's forgiving love based on his Word. They realized they could not go on living as victims. They had become victims of an "I Can't" mentality when they permitted the controlling group of people to have inordinate power over their lives.

Does some individual or group have that kind of power over you? Do you exercise it over others? Are any of the following attitudes familiar ones?

- Do as I tell you to do.

- Be what I tell you to be.

- Act as I tell you to act.

- Talk the way I tell you to talk.

- Dress as I tell you to dress.

- Suffer as I tell you to suffer.

- Believe as I say you should believe.

- Worship God as I say you should.

- Live your life as I tell you to live it.

- If you don't do as I tell you, you deserve to be punished.

Confidence Conquers Control

When a single mother I'll call Jane moved to a new state, she enrolled her children in what she thought was a good Christian school. The principal of the school had established rigid rules. One rule was that girls were not allowed to wear pants, not even under their skirts. So on cold rainy days the children were forced to slosh from building to building with their little legs getting cold and wet. Jane met with the principal. "My daughters are cold and wet!" she argued. She was told she was out of the will of God by not obeying the principal's authority.

On another occasion, one of Jane's daughters had worked hard preparing a report on the human ear. She planned to use a tape recorder as part of her presentation. But on the day of her report, she was put into detention for being caught with the tape recorder in her schoolbag.

Again Jane met with the principal, voicing her protest. Her daughter had been forced to sit in the school office all day as punishment. The girl had missed classes and had thereby gotten behind in her work. She was shamed in front of her friends.

The principal and his vice-principal stood before this Christian mother, and with shoulders squared and eyes ablaze they said, "Lady, you have to obey us like a wife obeys her husband." There was no sexual connotation in that admonition. What it meant was that she should shut up and do as she was told. The system was right, and it didn't matter how it damaged the children's health, their minds, their sense of self-esteem, or their spirits.

Jane's little daughter had to appear before a board of elders and ask forgiveness for her crimes of wearing pants under her skirt to school and carrying a walkman in her book bag. Imagine a child, barely taller than a desk, standing before ten glaring board members and confessing her sin of breaking the rules and then begging to be allowed to return to her classes.

Finally, this mother, who thought of herself as a basically shy and defenseless woman, marched to the school, demanded for the last time to see the principal, and announced she was withdrawing her children from the school permanently before any more damage was done them. We must realize how evil the controlling spirit is and what damage it does to our lives.

Exercises in Confidence

To help you step into the Dynamic of Confidence, here are five exercises to do as often as you wish.

1. Make a list of the events, experiences, and false teachings in your life that have diminished your sense of confidence.

2. Tell yourself, "My confidence is in Christ, not in experiences, whether the experiences are good or bad."

3. Tell yourself, "Though these experiences hindered and even wounded my sense of confidence, I can begin building a deeper and more solid confidence right at this moment."

4. Stop putting yourself down in any way whatsoever. Remove from your vocabulary "I'm so dumb" or "I'm so stupid," "so helpless," so whatever. If what you say about yourself is not *exactly* what the Lord Jesus says about you according to his Word, don't even think it!

5. You encourage and reward yourself when you remove yourself from ungodly controlling situations. Rejoice that the Dynamic of Confidence is at work in your life.

GOD SPEAKS:

Beloved,
You can never grow a garden
     if you continually trample on the seedlings.
You may choose not to change
     but soon the weeds
will twine around your neck
     and you will have to cut off your conscience
to go on.
     Others may seem to accept
your poor behavior,
     but thorns and stubble
mar your life
     where respect might have grown.
The full harvest of love
     demands respect;

and your need to control is not love.

When you wound another's heart,

that wound is

twice yours.

Be strong and of good courage,

my dear one.

Whatever you do,

do nothing out of fear.

I will be your confidence

forever.

PROVERBS 3:3; ROMANS 8:7;
GALATIANS 6:2,10; MATTHEW 7:16,20

Part Three

∞

Being There

7

The Dynamic of Achievement

∽

A chievement is defined as "a thing achieved by skill, work, and courage" and as "something that has been accomplished successfully, especially by means of exertion, skill, practice, or perseverance."

I like both of these definitions because they emphasize achievement as a thing *we* must do. Achievement doesn't just fall on us without any effort on our part. Achievement is quite different from success. Many people we think of as successful are simply famous or rich. Their gains may not have been gotten by efforts of skill, work, and courage. True success is found in *achievement*. Success by itself doesn't necessarily include achievement, but *achievement produces success.*

I don't believe rewarding and successful achievement can come before the other Dynamic Keys we've covered so far in this book. When our lives are centered in the Dynamics of Love, Solitude, Hope, Courage, and Confidence, we can exercise the Dynamic of Achievement in the way God meant for us to do. What we do is important to God.

Of course, success and achievement mean something different

to each of us. We move through our lives with individualized gifts and goals.

Suppose Susie declares herself to be a success because she not only married the man of her dreams but also landed the secretarial job she had always wanted. Susie's friend, Doris, happens to think her own ideal husband is a loser and her so-called "ideal job" is a dead-end nightmare.

Susie may, in spite of having the ideal husband and job, envy the success of Doris in other areas of life. Doris may be unemployed and six times divorced, but she may also be successful at losing ten pounds to fit into her jeans or making perfect yogurt from a culture. Success is subjective.

When I ask myself what success means to me personally, I might answer differently today than I would tomorrow. I know my answer a few years ago would not be the same as my response today. We are growing and learning every day. Our minds should grow along with our talents and strengths. Our spiritual lives should also be expanding in volume until we have no recourse but to explode with loving courage upon the world with our met goals and achievements. A question we should ask ourselves frequently—not just once or twice every few years—is "Do I consider myself a success? Why? (Why not?)"

Success Levels

There are several categories or levels of success. For women, the following four are the ones by which we tend to judge our success:

1: The Relationship Level—You may think you're a miserable failure or a great success depending upon how well you are handling your love life, your friends, and your family.

2: *The Work or School Level*—You may be right on target with your professional and scholastic goals and feel quite successful, or you may feel that because things are going badly, you are unsuccessful.

3: *The Personal Level*—You may feel quite successful because you're going to the gym every week, eating right, and spending time reading and enjoying life. In other words, you're living a balanced life and feel good about it. But on the other hand, if you are not taking care of these needs, you will lack a sense of control in your life.

4: *The Spiritual Level*—This is the most important level and the one most neglected. The Dynamic of Achievement needs to have its roots here. The other three levels of success will have little or no meaning unless our spiritual lives are in order. Intimacy with God, prayer, solitude, study of God's Word, and worship are the core from which all else evolves. "Success" is only a word if it is not born of the Spirit.

Goal-setting. It's rare to meet someone without any goals whatsoever. Goals may range from ones as simple as getting the refrigerator cleaned by Friday to running for President of the United States by 2012.

The "For Women Only" questionnaire at the end of this book asks, "Do you have goals in your life?" followed by the suggestion to list the most relevant ones. The questionnaire also asks, "When do you stop yourself from reaching your goals?" Most of the responses were based on fear. Many spoke of fear of rejection. Busyness and laziness were also causes of nonachievement.

A response that tugged at my heart was this one: "I stop myself from reaching my goals *all the time*. All the things I can't say no to occupy my time, so the important things I want to do are neglected. I know what I want to do and I know what I need to do—but I'm on a merry-go-round, and I honestly don't know how to get off."

This woman's response was typical of hundreds of others. The goals of many women are easily obscured by the busyness of life. We find it hard to focus on our goals.

The questionnaire asks, "Have you worked hard to earn love in your life?" and the answers have come thundering in at a resounding 99 percent saying "YES." And when I ask, "When you look at your life, can you say it's been 100 percent fulfilling?" the answers roar back: "No."

You can see by these responses that our energies are scattered. We confuse approval with achievement. We aren't sure why we aren't fulfilled. We work hard at earning approval, but it's a frustrating chore. We haven't spent enough time asking ourselves who we are, where we fit in the world, and why we do what we do and think what we think. We only *wish* for a higher life of accomplishment and achievement, but we don't permit ourselves the right to experience passage into lasting accomplishment and the fulfillment of our goals.

> Achievement is known by its character,
> not only by its appearance.

Four Women and Achievement

Here are four women and their dilemmas with achievement:

Lucy: Lucy is a hospital pharmacologist. Her husband was fired from his job as a lab technician in a local hospital due to a series of serious mistakes in the lab that cost the life of a misdiagnosed patient. As a result, Lucy's husband can't get another job in his field. Lucy knew her husband had problems, and now his careless-ness is obvious to others. There's little hope he will land a job as good as the one he sabotaged.

What should Lucy do? Her professional reputation is flawless. She's been offered a better job with higher pay in another hospital. She's accomplished and highly respected. However, Lucy is ner-vous about her own success and she is ashamed to tell her husband of her better job offer. She is afraid of going on to bigger achieve-ments when her husband has failed so badly. Lucy thinks her hus-band's problems are hers to solve. She is willing to lose all she has worked for to avoid her husband's jealousy or anger.

Camille: Camille is a bright high school student with an above-average IQ. She leads an active social life and is popular with boys. Her sister, who graduated from the same high school two years ago as the valedictorian, was not popular with boys and now attends a good university on a scholarship where she is in the top 5 percent of her class. She is still not popular with the boys. Camille is afraid if she succeeds in school she will be like her sister and boys won't be attracted to her. Her conclusion is, boys don't like girls who are too smart.

It doesn't occur to Camille to ask herself what kind of boys she wants to attract. She doesn't identify boys by their strength of character, their ability to bring out the best in others, or their sense of integrity, but by their simply *being* there. Camille thinks if she is too smart she will not be popular with boys in *general* and then maybe she'll be like her sister and wind up an old maid.

It does not occur to Camille to ask whether or not her sister is happy or fulfilled.

Elaine: Elaine is up for a promotion at work. It will mean managing a department of eight other workers where she will have to work harder and take more responsibility. Frayed with worry, she wonders if she should take the job. It offers a big pay raise, but oh, the responsibility! The effort! Does she want to pay the price for the achievement?

Ann: Ann is an artist who just corralled the interest of a prestigious gallery. She has been offered a one-person show of her work. This is a giant breakthrough in her career. To the dismay of her friends, she talks herself out of the show by finding a million things wrong with the gallery and the art dealer, sabotaging her success. Why?

Don't Sabotage Yourself

Sometimes achievement costs more than we are willing to pay. Others may resent you for your success. You may lose friends. Even family members can resent you if your achievements rise above theirs. Too often we sacrifice genuine fulfillment out of fear of failure and rejection.

On the other hand, the drive for achievement often runs hand-in-hand with the urge to fail. A woman may feel she is not good enough to achieve her goals. This feeling of inadequacy is like a blister on her foot. It doesn't go away no matter how staunchly she parades around in her best shoes. She can't feel good about the shoes because they hurt. Of course, the problem is not the shoes, it's the blister on her foot.

With the mistaken belief that she is not worthy of successful achievement, it doesn't matter how much a woman achieves, because down deep in her heart she believes she's worthless. With a feeling of unworthiness, she will unconsciously make sure she fails. If she does nothing to change, her life will continue to be a series of disappointments and frustration. She may not recognize the self-sabotaging acts she commits.

I've seen it too many times. Women sabotage themselves at the very point of success. They miss the important meeting, they wreck their cars, they get sick, they don't show up for work, they get involved in destructive relationships, they decide to change careers, they move to Bulgaria (or some other place to hide from themselves), they have an extramarital affair that brings disgrace and shame on themselves.

When a woman who is a pillar of society suddenly takes a plunge downward by stealing, cheating, lying, or some other sin, it doesn't make sense. She knows she'll get caught, and when she's caught, she will have sabotaged her position and standing in society. She will have let her negative opinion of herself become a self-fulfilling prophecy.

With an urge to fail, it stands to reason we will destroy the very achievements we should be managing with the greatest respect and care. Success can often be the first step toward failure because the achievement of success can make a person reactive, not creative. It is in the pure flow of creativity that our minds are the most free and elated. If the drive for achievement is not grounded in the joy and delight of *doing* and creating, we meet with discontent. And the discontent multiplies until it becomes overwhelming.

Risking love? Many women fear achievement because they are afraid they will no longer be loved by men. Nothing could be more ludicrous. The woman of Proverbs 31 was an achiever in all of the four levels of success—relational, professional, personal, spiritual—and she was called "blessed" by her husband.

A man who came to me for counseling with his wife asked me in complete despair, "Why is it women think they have to be weak in order for men to be strong?" What he longed for and needed was a strong woman at his side. Capable. Brave. A woman of confidence. What he had instead was a wife who lived her life as a little girl, hesitant to achieve too much because she was afraid maybe her big, strong man wouldn't love her anymore. This woman had fear mixed up with her Christian beliefs. Outwardly she was sweet and docile, yet inwardly she was driven by fear and a lack of confidence.

I heard this from an educated, accomplished woman: "I'm really a big fraud. I'm not as smart as people think I am. I don't really cut it with the people who are truly well-read and smart. I'm afraid they'll find out how dull-witted I really am."

This woman's deluded thinking had tied her in knots. She was in fact an intelligent woman, but she believed her achievements and abilities counted for very little. She feared others would find her out and then reject her. So naturally, she sabotaged her chances of becoming friends with people she would have found stimulating. Instead, she associated with people beneath her own abilities. She didn't realize how her wrong thinking was bruising her soul. Continually accepting less for ourselves always brings pain and hurts the soul. This woman's relationships were fraught with power struggles, arguments, impatience, and in the end, loneliness.

Shyness is not a virtue. Fear drives women into states of ungodly shyness. Narcissistic ideas and misbeliefs become guiding forces. We must realize that *shyness is not a virtue.* Look at the personality of God. You don't find shyness there. Look at the admonition of Jesus who tells us to be "strong and of good courage" and "filled with faith." There is nothing honorable or noble about shyness.

Children have the right to be shy because they are just beginning to learn their place in a world which looks very big in their eyes. But as grown-up women, we can look at the world through the eyes of wisdom and put aside childish ways.

Bring your self-doubt to the Lord in your solitude. Lay it at the foot of the cross. Then in the light of his Word, examine your misconstrued ideas about yourself and your place in the world.

At what price? What will achievement cost you? What consequences will you face if you accomplish success? Will your family still love you? Will you be corrupted by a sinful world? Will you lose the connection to people who are not as ambitious or capable as you? Will people be jealous of you, try to knock you off your pedestal? Will the competition be too cutthroat and fierce to handle? Will the stress of staying there be too much for you? Are you too sensitive to be able to handle criticism and ridicule?

You may find yourself avoiding achievement in order to keep yourself from pain. You may be so afraid of your achievements that you lose sight of the goals you have set for yourself. If this happens, your accomplishments will become diffused and life will seem more and more difficult for you. If you are afraid of the responsibility of achievement and success, you will, subconsciously, devise ways to cripple your dreams.

However, even if you let fear sabotage your success, you won't *forget* your dreams. You will remember them often, and you will feel frustrated and unhappy if they are unfulfilled. This is the point where a woman can develop an angry "I'll show you" attitude. She may become so bent on proving herself, and so frustrated at her nonachievement, that she comes out swinging at the world like a boxer in a ring. Now her attitude is not about achieving, it's more about revenge.

Who cares, anyhow? The truth is, the thrill of achievement fades quickly if your motives are to prove yourself to others. Nobody is ever as impressed with you as you imagine they should be. In fact, most people don't really care very much about what you do because they are more concerned with their lives than yours.

You think you'll get back at your father for the abusive way he treated you all your life. You'll show him, you think. Just wait until he sees your new car, hears you on the radio, comes to the big grand opening of your new whatever. You did it! You've arrived! There you sit on the top of your little mountain waiting for the accolades you so richly deserve and your father says, "So?" and proceeds to brag about your brother the bookie and your sister, who's in rehab at a detox center in Albuquerque.

Face it. You can never achieve enough to get the attention you think you deserve. The Dynamic of Achievement calls you to a place of power and ability that transcends your craving for attention and approval.

God sets you apart to hear from him and to know his will for your everyday activities. In your solitude you hear him speak to you of his love. You sense his goodness. You are energized and inspired. You develop confidence in who you are in him. You become courageous and daring. You try new things. You become willing to develop your gifts, which you then present back to God for his pleasure. Your entire motivation for achievement is to bring pleasure to God. All your achievements are for his pleasure.

Love, the Secret of Dynamic Achievement

If we place success above the need to love and be loved, we don't understand what success is all about. True success is living in God's love. God blesses us in all we do, and we experience his love in all our endeavors.

When we really want to bring pleasure to God, our achievements are born of love. We love what we do. If we write plays, our work is not about the success of the play. It is about the actual work of writing the play. The work becomes the reward.

My neighbor is hard at work planting a garden now. He has been working for days preparing the soil and getting ready for planting. He's taking his time and enjoying every minute of his work. I can see him out there in the sun whistling merrily and shoveling manure. At what point do you think he is an achiever? I'd say he's experiencing achievement and success every minute he spends at his task. He loves it!

When you plant a garden or paint the patio, do you experience achievement in the doing?

When Achievement Means Being the Best

I've counseled Hollywood personalities who, in spite of their fame, live on the edge of despair. Their achievements are shallow and empty because they are not infused with and inspired by love. The Dynamic of Achievement is born in the love of God.

These sad yet famous souls believe that if they are not the *best* at what they do, they are the *worst*. For them, being anywhere but on top is like being on the very bottom. Most of the people I've spoken with aren't even sure what being "on top" means. When we're flying high on a cloud, there can be that sneaky, insidious fear that there is nowhere to go but down.

The story line in the movie and stage production of *Sunset Boulevard* centers around the misled fictional character of an aging Norma Desmond, a former silent picture star who still believes she is a star. What a tragedy Norma Desmond's delusions represent! Here is a woman with everything—money, a rich and gilded past as the belle of silent films, a beauty that is still intact—but her mind is warped with the desire to fulfill what her definition of success was thirty or forty years ago. Decades have passed and she has remained a child. There is no room in her convoluted belief system to see how shallow the notion of "biggest and best" is, nor can she begin to opt for change. It doesn't occur to her to grab on to a new dream, a new pursuit. Her story is a mire of self-importance and deception.

Hollywood isn't the only place where not being the biggest and the best can be misinterpreted as failure. Though excellence is good, to some people a job well done is simply not rewarding enough. "Well done" can mean the same as failure. Like Norma Desmond, your opinions of yourself can depend totally on how much acclaim your achievements bring. If someone else appears to be more successful than you at what you do, you may be smitten with resentment and jealousy.

Emily Dickinson's statement "Success is counted sweetest by those who n'er succeed" rings true.

God's best. We have been created for God's pleasure. The Bible tells us in Ephesians 1:9 that according to his *pleasure* and will, we have been predestined as his adopted daughters through Jesus Christ. Psalms 149:4 tells us the Lord takes delight in his people. You and I are his delight.

The Lord lovingly explains that he will instruct us and teach us in the way we should go (Psalms 32:8). Our achievements are his achievements.

In Key #5, the Dynamic of Fullness, I said that our attitude must be that *we happen to life* instead of life happens to us. We don't just sit by as Christian women with the mistaken idea that "whatever happens, happens." Examine for a moment who you are right now. Remember how dearly God values your heart and soul. See inside your heart. Listen to the desire of your soul to bring pleasure to God. Look closely at yourself. See the immense treasure that resides within you. Tell yourself, *Where I am right now is the best place I can possibly be.*

Jesus has chosen your heart and soul to reflect his own by the power of his Spirit. The Spirit of God has been fused with your human spirit, permeating your soul and creating in you something beautiful. He moves into your heart and soul and patiently molds you into a likeness of himself. *He achieves his will in you, setting you free to achieve.* He performs the work in you and through you by his Spirit. He is instructing you in the way you should go. Willingly and confidently, you follow.

We are like trees planted by the rivers of water. We bring forth our fruit in season, and our leaves don't wither. Whatever we do prospers (Ps 1:1-3). We have committed all our works to the Lord because we love him with all our being. Our thoughts are firmly established in his truth (Prv 16:3). We are able to experience hardship and setbacks without considering ourselves failures and nonachievers.

We can, perhaps in a small way, understand the deep and profound meaning of Augustine's admonition to "love God and do as you please," for in Christ we live and move and have our being, and we no longer need be afraid of achievement and its consequences. We do not have to fear achievement and its responsibilities. Perfect love has cast out fear.

GOD SPEAKS:

Dearest flower,

by Me all matter is held together.

By Me the stars suspend in the heavens.

By Me the worlds were created.

By Me a new nature and a new person

were created in you.

You carry the banner of God within you.

You walk in My spirit.

You were created to bring pleasure

to Me.

There is no higher reward in this life

than the knowledge of my approval

and recognition.

The world may recognize you for what you DO.

You are recognized by Me for who you ARE.

I love your works. You bring me much pleasure,

when you respond to the leading of My spirit.

You will call upon Me for strength, courage,

and wisdom to perform each task

and I will always give you more than you ask.

Your achievements are My achievements.

Give back to Me, My dear one,

what I have given to you.

You may keep what is yours,

but give the glory to Me.

COLOSSIANS 1:16-18; JOHN 17:22

8

The Dynamic of Creativity

∞

The Holy Spirit blesses us with a childlike sense of wonder in the world around us and gives us the very mind of Christ to think with creative minds.

The necessary atmosphere for the development of our own creative abilities is living in the presence of God, the Divine Creator. You don't have to be smart to be creative, but you need a certain amount of expectancy and enthusiasm.

The Dynamic of Creativity depends upon each of the other nine keys in this book in order to function freely and beautifully in our lives. The Dynamic of Creativity depends on the Dynamic of Love and the Dynamic of Solitude to understand and follow God's leading.

No one can live a dynamic and confident life without creativity. We must not allow the cares of the world to interrupt the flow of creativity in our lives. The cares of the world will always interfere with our creative spirits if we allow them to. You make the decision to practice the piano, but suddenly you remember you should run to the bank or shampoo your hair or give the dog his medicine. You want to write in your journal, but instead you think of the phone calls you should make, the dishes in the sink, or some other chore.

Our talents are put on hold, untapped and unreleased while we busy ourselves with daily activities. Then at the end of the day we're so tired we sit down and watch television instead of developing and using our talents. We aren't even aware that the world outside our door is waiting for us to share our gifts.

To enter into the Dynamic of Creativity, we must return again to the Dynamic of Solitude. We enter that place to hear God's gentle voice guiding us. God longs to express himself through us creatively. All too often women will rush into creative endeavors that are exhausting or futile because they have not stopped to listen to God gently drawing out their true talents.

Listening to your own heart, meditating on God's Word, and allowing the Holy Spirit to inspire and direct you takes more than a few minutes a day or a week out of town once a year. Sometimes our lives are so packed with obligations that we live by rote and thereby starve our souls for creative expression.

A good exercise is to turn off your television, radio, CD player, tape recorder, anything that makes noise or is selling you something. Remove magazines and newspapers from your immediate environment. Then, without commercials and advertisements telling you what to buy, do, give, own, and be, reevaluate. Listen to your inner self.

What do you do when you are alone without the noise of popular culture assailing you? What do you think about when there are no outside influences to distract you? How do you choose your thoughts? How do you approach your trials? Do you think with vision? Are you a woman of hope? What words are you telling yourself? Remember, *life doesn't happen to you; you happen to life.*

Creativity, like the Dynamic of Hope, has its roots in vision. "Without vision my people perish" might be enlarged to mean that without imagination, vision, and hope we can perish inwardly. Both the Dynamic of Creativity and the Dynamic of Hope jump across the unknown onto new ground.

Being creative in our spiritual lives does not mean just outward expressions like bringing new instruments for worship, adding a new visual aid to the Bible study class you lead, or making banners for the church sanctuary. These are creative endeavors that are appreciated by everyone, but there is another kind of creativity.

Let me tell you a little fable to illustrate what a lack of creativity can do. You'll see where vision plays a role in the creative life. First, the story:

Fable of the Woman and Her View

Once there was a woman who lived in a house on the side of a hill. On the hill were many trees. One day the woman looked out the window and saw that a large branch had fallen from one of the trees and was blocking the view of her beautiful hill. She went outside and climbed the hill to remove the branch. As she climbed the hill a bee stung her foot. The woman forgot the branch and returned to the house to tend to the bee sting.

The next day a bird came along and made a nest in the fallen branch of the tree. The woman heard the bird singing and was surprised at the sound. She chose not to try to remove the branch that day.

A week later the woman decided to climb the hill to get a look at the bird's nest. She put her camera around her neck and started up the hill. On the way she fell and broke her arm. So she forgot about the bird in the fallen branch of the tree and returned to the house to get help for her broken arm.

The bird continued to sing in the tree. More birds joined the bird in the branch of the tree; the birds built nests and began laying eggs. Soon there were hundreds of birds singing on the woman's hill, and she could hear them chirping all day and all night.

The woman's broken arm healed and the bee sting went away. The singing of the birds became louder and louder as they grew in number. The woman grew tired of the song. It was not pleasant to her ears. She couldn't sleep at night, so she angrily closed the window tight and drew the blinds so she would no longer hear the birds' song.

The woman grew sad because her house was dark and quiet with the window covered and closed. She lamented that her hill was no longer the way it used to be. Then one day the singing suddenly stopped. The woman went outside and saw that the branch had lost all its leaves. She saw that the birds had flown away. The dead branch lay on the side of the hill, bent and dry like a crooked bone.

The woman climbed the hill and removed the dead branch with all its empty birds' nests. She opened her window again. She looked forward to having the view of her hill once again.

But the hill was not the same. There was an empty spot where the branch had been before she removed it. The hill was different now. It wasn't as beautiful as it had been before. The woman became even more depressed.

The sky was dull and empty without the fluttering of the birds. Bees moved into the empty spot where the branch had fallen. The days and nights were long and still.

The woman rubbed her arm where it had been broken. She scratched her foot where the bee had stung. She pulled on her ear that had heard the song of the birds. She was so sad she stopped looking out the window.

Then one night the woman was awakened by something staring at her. Something stared, direct and steady, straight at her. She sat up erect in bed and drew the covers to her chin.

The window was open. Outside her window in the moonlight were the hill and its trees. They seemed to be alive. They seemed to peer in her window, looking directly at her. The woman hid her head under the covers. It was very, very quiet.

Interpreting the fable. The woman in the fable illustrates several points. If we look closely, we'll see ourselves in her. First we see a problem (the broken branch), and we want to fix it, get rid of it, remove it. The thing that is wrong—broken—destroys our view of a lovely and orderly world. We want things orderly, predictable, neat, and the same. In the story, the view of the hill was lovely and it made the woman happy. She didn't want her happiness disturbed.

But when the branch broke and fell, the woman was disturbed. She wanted things as they were. So she immediately set off up the hill to remove the branch. (Notice, the removal of the problem requires a climb. Problem-solving is never a downhill slide. It's always a hard climb upward.) The woman was on her way up the hill, and what hapened? She was stung by a bee and couldn't go on. The bee sting was significant. She was stung by life. She was trying to do something she thought was good and what happened? She got stung! Her plight was put on hold and she returned to her house discouraged.

Out of the problem, however, comes something lovely. A song. The problem hadn't been fixed, but there was a song in it. Not only was there a song, but there was new life.

Problems, intrusions, interruptions, trials—all hold an important message within themselves—something we need to listen to. We need to begin to respect our problems (instead of dreading them). For out of our problems we will not only find a new song but new life.

But the woman didn't think of such things, so off she went up the hill again, this time to get a look at the bird's nest, perhaps even photograph it. The problem had given birth to music, but she didn't understand the music. She expected to capture the moment on film. What happened? She broke a bone.

It's significant that it's a bone the woman broke because bones are what hold human beings together. A bone implies something hard and strong. So, *again*, she was stopped in her tracks when she had set out to do something good. Should we retreat in defeat when life is unfair? Or should we honor our wounds and give homage to the process of mending? Should we be bitter when we find a song in our problems only to meet with more problems?

Bones heal and bee stings go away. But the woman learned very little from the mishaps she experienced. She encountered a "too-much-of-a-good-thing" problem and could no longer tolerate the singing of the birds. It became monotonous to her. It was just too much for her ears, so what did she do? She entered into a state of denial and slammed the window closed. She did nothing to create an agreeable solution. Instead, she pulled the covers over her head and ignored the problem that faced her. The singing had not gone away; she just couldn't hear it because she had blocked out its sound.

Her denial robbed her even further. She did not get to experience the rewards of facing the intrusion—the problem—head-on.

The intrusion represents what too much of a good thing can do to us, and how we can allow ourselves to be numbed by lack of vision. The woman enjoyed a small dose of music but became frustrated when the songs of the birds were out of her control. We, too, want to maintain control.

In the woman's state of denial and the absence of creative vision, she placed herself in darkness. The darkness depressed her. She was trapped where she lived, imprisoned in her own home, without light.

But then the music stoped. She flung open the window and saw another broken bone, like her own: the branch of the tree lying useless. Its brokenness was without music. Now she removed it. She had control over the helpless thing since it's far easier to manage something when it puts up no struggle, so she hauled the dead log from the hill. Was she happy at last? No.

Then there was an empty place where the trouble once was. Emptiness was as real as fullness. So into the emptiness came the bees which had once stung her and would sting again. They took over. Characteristically, the woman ignored the bees, choosing not to recognize that they would multiply.

The woman looked at her view from the window. She saw the hill she once took pride in. But it was not the same now. Without vision to celebrate change, to value the places that have been broken in our lives and our world, we are left with disappointment and a stunted awareness of the real world.

The woman didn't realize that the lesson of the hill with its birds, bees, broken limb, and song had been a gift to her. She wanted things to be as they were before the troubles.

The world is simply not the same after you have listened to its music. Problems and trials leave us changed, whether we know it or not. The world is not the same after you've felt life's sting or snapped a bone. These experiences can give you a new, fresh, more mature view, or like the woman in the story, our life experiences can pass by, unexamined and unloved. We become imprisoned by our desire for things to remain the same. "Why can't things be like they were in the old days?"

So the woman went to bed but was awakened in the night, not by the sound of singing but by a steady stare of something big and terrible. It alarmed her, and she pulled up her covers over her head to hide from whatever it was, and she told herself, "I'll protect myself from this thing by pretending it's not there." We see her denial and lack of vision.

In the quiet of the moonlight, the hill waited outside the woman's window, watching her. Its eye was a steady, constant one that does not blink or close. The woman, who had only *reacted* to the hill's beauty and had never truly engaged herself in its life, was now the object of the *hill's* gaze.

She could not touch her world, so the world touched her. She could not happen to life, so life happened to her.

She has become the view.

Rising above the Superficial

My story of the woman and the hill is not about right and wrong. The woman really didn't do anything overtly *wrong*. After all, she started out just wanting to get rid of a dead branch so she could see the view from her window. What's wrong with that?

I am saying that everything in your life speaks to you, and if you live on a superficial plane, seeing only the obvious, asking little of your sufferings other than that they go away, you'll miss out on some of the most precious lessons the soul can learn. *Life will happen to you. You won't happen to life.*

I am suggesting we rise above a superficial walk through life. You may love helping people, but even this can be superficial. The blood of Jesus bathes our souls and washes the superficial out of us, and we find ourselves less and less vexed by anxiety, fear, worry, anger, backbiting, faultfinding, and petty quarreling (all symptoms of the superficial).

The Upward Climb

It may seem like an upward climb, but we can make our everyday lives creative. We move a step up every time we choose to creatively handle situations and tasks at hand. We can make even the act of sweeping the floor a creative expression.

Personally, I find doing the laundry a creative task which I take pleasure in. I like the smell of the detergent. I like the sound of the washing machine, the softness of the clothes when I pull them out of the dryer. My family's clothes are precious to me because my family is precious to me. I have a sense of satisfaction in the task as I pray for those who will wear the clothes, use the towels, sleep on the sheets.

Think of the everyday tasks you perform that until now you've considered low on the ladder of importance. Now imagine each task as a creative expression of yourself. Washing the car, buying groceries, making the bed, polishing your shoes—these are not meaningless tasks, they are the upward climb that can sweeten your creative mind if you allow them to. The activities that fill your days have the power to lift you to new heights of creative expression.

We make a mistake when we categorize our work obligations as necessary drudgeries. That frame of mind only helps us to shift into automatic pilot as we go about "getting things done," but without enjoyment or pleasure.

Finding the Creative in the Mundane

I once had a job typing mailing labels eight hours a day for a publisher in New York. It had to be one of the most boring jobs on the planet. All day long I sat there typing names and addresses in a room without windows. I realized that if I was going to survive the tedium I had to somehow make the job fun for myself, so I invented a new game every day as I typed. How many labels a minute? How many names starting with M? How many French names? Italian names? Jewish names? How many from Michigan, Minnesota, and so on? I became a rather fast typist through the experience.

Attitudes count more than we think. *Your attitude creates artfulness.* And artfulness expresses more of yourself than you think. The soul feeds on life's experiences and digests them, creating character. Don't rob yourself. Nourish yourself with creative and emotionally satisfying experiences. Even in mundane tasks, release your creative nature to make the difference between boredom and a genuine experience of discovery.

I'll never forget one of my first jobs as a teenager. It was the Christmas season and my best friend, LaRee, and I dressed in our most businesslike clothes and went to downtown Minneapolis to apply for sales clerk jobs at Dayton's department store. We considered the job of salesclerk to be quite glamorous, so we were at our very nervous best as we filled out the application forms and went through the interview process. LaRee landed the coveted and exciting salesclerk job, but I was hired as an *elf* in Santa Land.

My job was to inflate the balloons Santa handed out, so I was given a little stool and placed in a storeroom behind Santa's throne. It was the nightmare of my existence.

Not only was LaRee "out on the floor" among people and

wondrous activity, she came to work prettily dressed in her street clothes. I sat hunched in my red pointy hat and an elf's suit behind boxes of toys in a dimly lit, hot, stuffy storeroom. Once every half-hour or so I emerged into the light, elflike, to hand Santa a new bouquet of balloons to give to the children. I would exclaim, "Meeerry Christmas, boys and girls!" in a squeaky elf voice and return to the storeroom to inflate more balloons.

What's worse, LaRee would come by on her exciting breaks from her exciting salesclerk job and chuckle wildly as I jingled past in my little elf costume handing out balloons.

I didn't think there was a way on earth to make such a job interesting. Furthermore, I didn't *want* to make it interesting. I was, you might say, creatively challenged. Even now when I am reminded of those dreaded weeks at the helium tank blowing up balloons hour upon hour, I remember the eternity of every minute, and the certain feeling I was doomed to everlasting perdition wearing jingle bells and a red pointy hat, and being swallowed in a sea of balloons.

Loving Your Creativity

When we have reverence for what we touch, say, feel, taste, and do, the everyday matters of our lives take on value. William Saroyan said, "If you want to behold a truly religious man in action, go to Fresno and watch a farmer watering his trees, vines, and plants."

Tend to your activities with as much care as that farmer who loves his plants and vines. Visualize your work as a means of entry into a higher spiritual activity rather than merely a means to superficial rewards such as money, acclaim, and the appearance of success.

Living beyond the ordinary means to engage in imagination, playfulness, and curiosity, as we experience each day. I think of the little character in my children's books, Alula-Belle Button-Top Paintbrush Soft Shoe Poocheeni Magrew, who tells her friend, "The wind is a friend of mine," and then as the wind blows a gust their way, Alula-Belle explains, "The wind is always blowing kisses. If people checked with their noses more often, they'd realize that."

Maybe we ought to check with our noses more often. If you don't feel the wind like a kiss, maybe to you the wind is just the wind. A rose is just a rose. The ocean is just the ocean. A job is just a job.

When you choose to live beyond the ordinary, nothing is *just* an anything. A friend of mine whose work is insurance sales was asked to help out in an Italian restaurant at the cash register while the owner went to Italy for a few days. The owner was in a jam and needed someone he trusted to handle the money for him while he was gone. The restaurant owner was a close friend of my acquaintance, so my friend couldn't refuse. He agreed, although not without trepidation. "What do I know about cashiering?" he pondered. "Besides, I don't have time."

To encourage him, several of us went to the restaurant for dinner one night. What we found was astonishing. The place was packed with people, and our friend was singing Neapolitan songs, dancing, serving food on trays, and telling jokes, all while ringing up bills and taking in the money at the cash register. "I decided to have fun at this," he told us. The customers loved his gentle and amusing entertainment, the waiters were delighted as the tips rolled in, and the owner made money. Everyone was happy.

As we walked to our car in the parking lot outside the restaurant, we could still hear our friend inside bellowing out "O Sole Mio" to a table of four at the window beside the cash register.

What Is Talent?

Does creativity imply talent? What is "talent" anyway? How do you know if you're a talented person? Have you given yourself the opportunity to discover your gifts and abilities? Do you think that maybe you have no particular gifts? I know someone who considers herself talented because she can talk louder and longer than anyone else.

Usually we think of talent in terms of comparison. We look at ourselves and what we can do to see if we measure up to someone else's performance. If we evaluate ourselves as OK compared to others, we are more likely to develop our talents further.

Too often we underrate ourselves, underestimate our abilities, and undermine our gifts. In my work as a writer I interview dozens of people every year, many of them celebrities and many of them profound achievers. Recently, in a private interview, I asked a famous comedienne from a popular TV series the question, "What do you think you do best?" There was a long pause. Naturally I figured she'd say something about having the ability to make people laugh. But no. She sighed, fumbled for words, and then said apologetically, "Probably I don't do anything really well."

Talent and Discipline

One of my teachers once said there is no shortage of talent in the world, but there is a definite lack of discipline. I think we have to add that a major ingredient to the development and free expression of talent is *confidence*.

A beginning art student learns to draw the same thing over and over again until it is satisfactorily rendered. This is a discipline—

structured training. It is a training that corrects, molds, and perfects. Paul says in 1 Corinthians 9:25, "Everyone who competes in the games goes into strict training." It is an attitude of life we need to adopt. We discipline our minds, our attitudes, the concerns of our hearts, and the fruit of our lives. The fruit of our lives is our creativity and our talents.

Discipline is required to break the habit we've acquired of putting off today what we think we'll do tomorrow. Discipline is needed in every area of our lives if we are to be confident women. See your life as a work of art, with many colors, many dimensions, many textures. *Practice* this awareness.

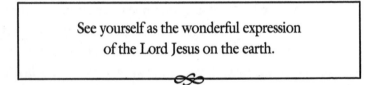

See yourself as the wonderful expression
of the Lord Jesus on the earth.

We don't have confidence if we don't think what we do has significance. If an accomplishment is too easy, we feel undeserving of respect. So one message we need to give ourselves is "Look for the challenge."

Number one on our list, then, in learning to know our talents is to *recognize* what's easy for us and what isn't and how we feel about both. Secondly, we need to see ourselves as talented women. If your opinion of yourself is that you really can't do anything well, that's the prophecy you'll live out and fulfill.

Fail with Flair!

The Dynamic of Creativity leaves no room for worries about failure. This fear will squelch even the most promising talent. I tell women everywhere to dare to fail. Think for a moment. Was it worries about failure or inadequacy that persuaded you to give up your piano lessons? To drop out of college? To quit studying Hebrew?

Worrying about doing a bad job or mucking things up is a dead end. It robs your soul of the joy of discovery. It snuffs out the fruit of your creative nature. It levels a gray pall on your beautiful creative spirit.

If you're going to fail, do it with *flair* and then—and this is the key—go on and do it again. And again. And again. Don't let anything stop you. Remember what you learned when we studied the Dynamic of Achievement. The Lord longs to express *himself* in you. If you make a mess of a flower arrangement or miss notes while playing a flute recital or slip on a dance step, give all to the Lord. He loves it all. Not just a nice end result.

Return to the Key of the Dynamic of Fullness. Reread the section about the cup that is filled to overflowing. God's only requirement is that you be filled. Protect your heart and soul from the greasy fingerprints of worry and fear.

Repeat out loud the following statements:

- I am a creative person.

- I give myself permission to try new things.

- I do not have to do all things well.

- I give myself permission to fail.

- If I fail, I choose to fail with *flair*.

Release Your Creativity

You don't have to paint the Sistine Chapel or write *Leaves of Grass* to be a creative person. To be fully alive is to participate in the creative process. Whatever route your life takes, let it be creatively expressed. As a salesperson, allow your creative instincts to flower. As a housewife, actor, musician, computer analyst, waitress—whatever your endeavor or work, allow your imagination and intuitive energy its expression.

Christians should be the most creative people in the world. Talent with a capital *T* in our lives is the Holy Spirit himself. He gives us the very mind of Christ so we may think creatively. God moves in each of our lives in uniquely different ways. My path is not the same as your path. My message may not be the same as yours.

In order to release your creativity and discover your talents, here's a prescription for your inspection and thought:

1. *Accept* the fact that you are precious to God, perfectly formed, and given an abundance of talent waiting to be released.

2. *Realize* that to develop your talents, it means you'll be spending time alone. It is in the Dynamic of Solitude that you hear God speak most clearly. This is the place from which creativity springs.

3. *Discipline.* Many would-be creative persons won't submit to the rigor of learning techniques and practicing discipline and logical thinking. We cannot ignore the fact that even such people as Giotto, da Vinci, and Einstein had teachers.

When I embark on a new painting or a new book, play, story, or poem, I don't think about whether it will be good or not. I try not to worry if anyone will appreciate my work, accept it, or consider what I do in any way important. The same is true for me when I sing a song or snap a photograph or arrange the pillows on the sofa or vacuum the carpet.

Questions I *never* ask are "Who will appreciate me?" and "Do I have talent?" I am confident in my place in the kingdom of God. From the first moment many years ago when I realized that our work brings pleasure to the Lord, my creative life took wing.

In the survey I conducted for this book, I asked the question, "When do you feel closest to God?" One lady responded, "When I'm up in the mountains! When I'm hiking or skiing, alone with God. I feel so alive in the mountains!"

This is a creative answer from a woman who lives her life in touch with nature. Perhaps she finds her truest self in the quiet of nature. Perhaps that is where she meets God in solitude.

According to Genesis 1:28-31, the world is ours to take care of and appreciate. It is ours to nurture and be nurtured by. "I feel so alive in the mountains!" is a beautiful statement because it expresses the jolt of wonder and enthusiasm we experience when immersed in the creativity of God. Because the woman in the fable didn't see her reflection in nature, nature could only stare blankly back at her.

Living beyond the ordinary is finding the place where you are truly *alive*.

You are always in the act of creating
—whether aware of it or not.

Whatever you are doing, do it heartily, confidently. Attitudes and ideas create the art the hand produces. The words you tell yourself will determine the joy of your work. When you tell yourself, "This may not be the most pleasant situation in the world, *but I can make it interesting for myself*," you'll see a big change take place. My insurance salesman friend, who was quite leery about cashiering, turned the experience into an event. People are still talking about it.

The Bad News about Fitting In

It seems pathetic to me when Christian women hurl their gifts to the wind just to fit in with a group. Take my friend Carol, for example (not her real name, of course). She is a colorful character, loves art and literature, poetry and music. She has a particular passion for the music of Vivaldi and Telemann.

When Carol became involved in a church, the pastor and the other leaders ridiculed the interests Carol loved, admonishing her to abandon such "carnal" and useless pursuits. The people Carol wanted to please weren't readers of literature or poetry and never developed an interest in baroque music. Carol obviously didn't fit in, but she loved the Lord and wanted to serve him. She came to believe God wasn't interested in the same things she was, even though her interests enhanced her life and made her a more fulfilled and confident Christian.

I saw Carol a couple of weeks ago, and she didn't appear to be much like Carol to me. Her *joie de vivre* was missing. Her face was set with a grim expression. Even the way she dressed was without her usual panache. "I'm serving God," she said in a stern voice.

Carol's need for approval was so great she didn't realize God would never require her to become someone else before she could serve him. Being Carol was just fine. I hope she will find herself again one day.

Remember the stinging bees in the "Fable of the Woman and Her View"? The stress of earning approval stings the soul like bees. It is exhausting and noncreative. It makes an automaton of you and robs you of discovering your full potential. The Dynamic of Love promotes and encourages you. The Dynamic of Fullness shows you your potential. The Dynamic of Creativity gives your life its brightness and color. It is the most joyous of the keys to a confident and dynamic life. It's the most fun.

When you live your life creatively, and you accomplish your work with a creative spirit, you are essentially partnering with God in his work. When you engage in creative acts like making something with your hands, repairing something to a working condition, building something—whether it be a bigger clientele or an office complex—you are essentially working with God in the creation of a world.

GOD SPEAKS:

The measure of life you bring to your world
  is the measure of your creativity.
  I bring light to your mind,
I refresh your energies,
  I bring you to your truest, holy self
where your creativity resides.

How painstakingly the artist trains her hand
  to record the world as seen through her eyes,
how long and arduous are the hours the musician
  practices to form the sounds notated
by the soul's music,
  and how endless is the writer's task
to record in words the language of the heart.
  Yet all belongs to God.

All is, and all was,
  and all will be Mind.
Creativity is bonding your soul
  with Mine.

      LUKE 9:23; JOHN 15:5

9

The Dynamic of the Physical Body

∞

This chapter will look at the way we think about our bodies, and secondly, how we treat our bodies. To most women, appearance means more than health—until something goes wrong, that is. When something goes wrong with our bodies, we become obsessive in our efforts to get well again.

It's rare to meet a woman who doesn't want to look her best. At this time in history and in this country especially, we women have the luxury of making ourselves as outwardly beautiful as we have the time and energy to give to the pursuit of beauty. The Little Girl Woman is particularly obsessed with her looks (review Key #5, the Dynamic of Fullness). The Little Girl Woman wants to stay pretty and adorable at all costs.

American women may be more beautiful than ever outwardly, but I have discovered in speaking with thousands of women across this country that we don't understand or truly treasure our bodies. I am amazed at the number of women I encounter who don't listen to or value their bodies. They simply don't care, as long as it looks good and functions well.

The perfect body. If we are buying a bouquet of flowers for someone, we expect the florist to give us the nicest bouquet for our money. We expect the fruits and vegetables we buy at the supermarket to be fresh and unspoiled. We expect the clothes we buy to be sewn properly, with no tears or stains. We want the house we buy to be upright and not falling down. We want the car we buy to be in perfect running condition. We want our friends and loved ones to be true and faithful, our leaders to be just and walk with integrity. What do we expect of our bodies?

Some of us have more physical problems than others. One of my good friends has lived most of her life in a wheelchair. She does not think of herself as a weak or helpless woman although she has lost count of the numerous surgeries she has had to undergo just to stay alive. She gives her body daily to God as her gift to him. Her desire is to bring God pleasure in every area of her life, including her physical body. She thinks of herself as altogether beautiful, as we read in the Song of Solomon. She serves God with all her heart, soul, and body. It is what God asks of each of us. She is content with her situation.

Perfect contentment. I think of the words of Paul, "I have learned in whatsoever state I am in, therewith to be content" (Phil 4:11, KJV).

Contentment? Yes. And contentment takes work, just as confidence and happiness take work; and for the most part, love also takes work. Of course, we don't work for God's approval, as each key in this book emphasizes. We understand we are saved by the unmerited favor of God toward us and not by our own works. It is our willingness to please God that is so very precious to him. Romans 12:1 tells us to present our bodies to God as living sacrifices. In your solitude each day, choose to be content with your body, and then be willing to give your body as a gift to God.

You Can Be a Living Sacrifice

When I read the lives of the saints of the early church, I am taken with their courage and also their willingness to suffer physically for their faith. They considered their bodies to be gifts to God. They shared a disdain for riches and comforts and chose suffering and deprivation in order to maintain their faith and preach the truth to others. Hundreds of these brave men and women were martyred, and they went to their deaths without a struggle, praising the Lord for the enormous privilege of giving up their bodies to God.

Women martyrs abound. Women were beheaded for their faith in Christ. They were torn to pieces by lions, stoned, burned alive, beaten, drowned, boiled, thrown in the sewer, butchered. All, like Joan of Arc, died praying, praising God, singing songs of faith, and proclaiming their faith in Christ for their tormentors to hear.

When I realize how these great men and women suffered, I am humbled. Our lives seem like an endless birthday party when placed beside their lives of torment and early death. For proclaiming their faith in Christ, they were tortured and murdered. Most of us do not have to face such a test.

What a price these great Christians paid for the fires of our faith to go on burning through the ages. Suppose they had all recanted and slunk away into the shadows of oblivion? Our history would be tragically altered.

Treasure in earthen vessels. How much do we treasure the gifts God gives us today? How much do we value our saved souls? How much do we treasure our bodies? Do we consider our bodies as gifts to God?

In March of 1997, when news of more than forty suicide deaths in Rancho Santa Fe, California, reached the world, it aroused universal shock and disgust. A cry of outrage came from the appalled nation. How could people be so deceived as to willingly take their own lives for some bogus cult notion? Their suicide notes explained how happy they were to be shedding their miserable shells of bodies.

When we hate our bodies and believe they are mere shells to be despised, we are capable of any madness. The gnostic belief that our bodies are evil is far from what God tells us.

On Easter Sunday at our church this year the boys' and girls' Sunday school classes gave a little program that began with two boys carrying a large, vine-covered cross down the center aisle of the sanctuary. The cross was placed in the middle of the stage, and when the presentation ended, there were blooming flowers in the vines. The two boys then carried off the flower-decked cross.

I was gripped with the image of that flowery cross. I thought immediately of our gifts to him. Isn't that what we do every day? Place our lives, like flowers, on the cross as gifts to God? "Present your bodies as a living sacrifice...."

In the first century Ignatius was thrown to the lions at the Coliseum in Rome, and before eighty thousand spectators he was ripped to bits and eaten. Here is what he said before going into the ring to his horrible death: "The only thing I ask of you is to allow me to offer the libation of my blood to God.... I am the wheat of the Lord.... Caress then, these beasts, that they may be my tomb."

When I read these words, I ask myself how I can honor God by *living*. Chances are you and I will not die in the teeth of lions for our faith. Shall I be less brave in *living* than these heroes were in dying?

Jesus himself died like a wretched criminal on the cross. The beatings he received were cruel and inhuman. Scripture tells us he was so badly beaten that his face was not even recognizably human: "His appearance was so disfigured beyond that of any man and his form marred beyond human likeness" (Is 52:14). Now we pray, "Lord, let your face, *the face that was brutalized and disfigured*, shine upon me."

The Lord Jesus suffered a terrible, shameful death so that we can live forgiven and free Spirit-filled lives in his strength. His face was bloodied and ruined so that our faces might reflect his love. His body was beaten and tortured so you and I can live in bodies that are blessed as gifts to him. He was killed for our sakes so we will not die, but live eternally.

Respect for Our Bodies

If we continually remind ourselves that the Lord loves us and our bodies, we may begin to respect our bodies with new gratitude. Jesus died to redeem our souls, spirits, *and* our bodies.

Our bodies themselves seem to be giving us mixed messages. In the many books, videos, and tapes I've produced and written on health and fitness, including the *Free to Be Thin* books with Neva Coyle, two questions prevail: "What does *God* think of my body?" and "Does he care?"

The "For Women Only" questionnaire has the question, "When do you feel most lovable?"

Almost every second response read, "I feel most lovable when I am *thin*."

However, in response to another question, "Name some women you admire and hold as role models in your life," not one of the answers included *thin* women as role models *because* they were thin.

So what are we saying?

In our latest book, *The All-New Free to Be Thin Lifestyle-Plan*, we present the mirror test. We suggest finding a full-length mirror and looking into it. Can you say the following words out loud to yourself?

- I am fearfully and wonderfully made.

- I accept myself.

- I accept and bless my body.

- I will eat and care for my health because I am precious.

- I choose not to abuse myself in any way.

- My body was created to be healthy, and I will cooperate with God to make it so.

Free to be Thinners learn to be thankful for their bodies, no matter what shape they're in. We pray like this:

> Heavenly Father, I thank you for my body. I thank you for creating me exactly the way you did. Show me how to take care of this precious body you have given me. I choose to bless my body because you love me with an everlasting love. You have fearfully and wonderfully made me, and I thank you.

Appreciation for your body. God speaks to each of us individually. He speaks to me about my physical body in a way he doesn't speak to you about your physical body. We are unique individuals. David sang, "You created my inmost being; you knit me together in my mother's womb. I praise you because I am fearfully and wonderfully made" (Ps 139:13-14). Each of us is fearfully and wonderfully made. Do we respect this creation of ourselves? Do we offer ourselves in all our fearful wonderfulness back to God?

Concern about the way we look is shared by almost every twenty-first century woman. We care about our weight, our hair, our nails, our clothes, our skin—essentially how others perceive us. Most of our personal care is not out of appreciation for ourselves and the way we were knit together, but out of pressure to compete with other women.

If you want to make yourself miserable in a hurry, just read secular women's magazines. You'll see very quickly how you don't measure up. I recently visited the dentist and, in about a half an hour, I read more self-defeating material than I'd seen in a whole year. I read about the "disaster areas on my body"; how I need to look younger and combat the stages of aging if I am to compete in today's youth culture; how I'm really not the cook I should be if I don't prepare quail with plum sauce; how we women only make sixty-six cents to every man's one dollar; and why my fingernails won't really send out a message unless I'm aware of something called "nail power."

There were several articles on how to win and keep a man and why I'm not alluring enough for today's sexual revolution. Every magazine I picked up had a "shed pounds NOW" diet plus a few full-color pages of a glamorously in-shape female doing "get in shape NOW" exercises. The message we are supposed to receive is "I have a problem if I'm not as thin, clever, talented, or in shape as these photos."

By the time I was called to see the dentist, I was sure I was a hopeless victim of flab and bad nails, a shamefully bad cook and sweetheart, and absolutely inept at earning a living.

When I tell women to be good to their bodies it almost sounds glib. Some women take my teaching as self-centered or vain. (God forbid! Laying ourselves on the altar of Christ is hardly self-centered.)

Discipline. To be good to our bodies takes discipline. When it comes to the body, the challenge of discipline is obvious. It is as necessary as the discipline we discussed in the Key of the Dynamic of Achievement. You can harbor a bad thought for days and your bus driver won't be particularly aware of it. But if you eat a pound of chocolates every day, soon everyone on the bus will see your lack of discipline.

Lack of discipline leads to frustration and self-loathing. I've never met an undisciplined person who was truly delighted with life. Discipline is necessary for your happiness. It is necessary for your confidence. Your soul craves your acts of discipline.

Sometimes your own body and emotions create snares for you. You become frustrated by situations over which you feel you have little or no control, and your discipline flies out the window. "I ate the birthday cake because nobody showed up at the party." "I'm just too busy to exercise." Cheryl tells me she overeats because her husband overeats. She is then able to blame her action on something other than herself, and in that way avoid feelings of guilt.

Discipline takes patience. My favorite example of patience comes from a poem written by Jack Meyers called "Doing and Being." He describes patience like that of the raven, who once every hundred years appears with a silk scarf in its beak and drags it lightly over the mountaintop, and in this way gradually wears the mountain down.

Patience is a friend of discipline. You need them both as you gradually wear the mountain down.

Responsibility is also a friend of discipline. Maybe you hate taking responsibility for your body because you can't or don't want to identify your needs. (Reexamine the Basic Needs List in Key #5, the Dynamic of Fullness.) When we are frustrated and unhappy we punish our bodies. Discipline, or self-control, and patience teach us to be responsible for seeing our own needs are met so we are not frustrated and unhappy. Our cruelty to our bodies is an act of emotional irresponsibility.

Why Do We Hurt Our Bodies?

Cheryl, the woman I mentioned earlier, has inordinate needs for her husband's approval. She believes that if she dutifully eats the way he eats, including eating foods that are clearly dangerous to her health, he will see what a good wife she is. Cheryl has several allergies, including a severe allergy to milk products. But if her husband has a yen for ice cream, Cheryl will join him in his indulgence and suffer later.

Needs for acceptance, needs for a sense of security, needs for friendship and love, needs for productivity, and a feeling of being necessary in the lives of others are all important needs. They are needs that we must not deny.

We are responsible to see to it that these needs are met in our lives. Nobody on earth is responsible for our needs but we ourselves. Examine your needs again to see how they relate to the care of your body:

The need for approval. You should have approval in your life. You should have enough reinforcing, energizing, and encouraging people and activities around you so that you feel a sense of confidence in your choices.

Without these in place you may reach for other reinforcers that essentially hurt your body as well as your soul. You may overeat, consuming foods that are high in fat and sugar, or you may drink alcohol in an effort to numb the feelings of loneliness. You will more than likely not exercise. You may overwork in an effort to fill your hours with pain-numbing activity.

The need for a sense of security. You can't be truly content without feeling you are safe and secure. It is imperative you take responsibility and create a sense of security for yourself. If you have lost your job, your home, your husband, your savings, you have need for a renewed sense of security.

A writing student of mine lost her home in a neighborhood fire last year, and she lost everything she had spent a lifetime building. Thankfully she and her family escaped the fire unharmed, but nothing else survived, not a dish, not a pen, nothing. Her sense of loss was enormous.

Immediately we began working together on her next writing project. She began building her life again, this time without the comfort and security of her beautiful home filled with heirlooms and family treasures.

Our security is in Christ. Once we have settled the fact that he is our security and our safety, we can begin to build our earthly places of safety. Home should be a place of security. We should have a sense of pride and pleasure in the place we live. If we do not, we will envy others what they have. We might translate this envy into self-punishment in the way we neglect to take responsibility for our bodies, stuffing ourselves on bread and pastries just to feel full and satisfied.

The need for friendship and love. I've seen more suffering in the lives of people due to this need being unfulfilled than any other. If this need is not satisfactorily met, we will make friends of things such as chocolate, wine, food, cigarettes, indiscriminate sex. The time to make sure you have encouraging, uplifting friends in your life is *now*. Too often we bruise our souls with hurtful relationships.

"Oh, Max loves me," sighs a woman I'll call Edith. "I know he loves me because he won't let me drive a car, and he won't allow me to work. I don't have girlfriends because my Max wants me all to himself. We don't have other friends because Max wants to spend all our free time alone together. Isn't that love?"

Max isn't displaying love, he's a full-fledged controller (see Key #6) who mistakes possessing a woman for loving her. Love doesn't imprison us, love sets us free. Love lifts us up and helps us reach our full potential.

Edith, with her need for love and friends unmet, punishes herself in several ways. Physically, she starves herself, trying to stay slim and attractive for Max. All she eats is a cantaloupe a day and ten raisins. She also smokes two packs of cigarettes a day.

The need for productivity and a feeling of being necessary in the lives of others. If you deny this need, you may find yourself placing unfulfilling activities in your life where true productivity belongs. You won't particularly like the way you spend your days. You may feel restless, bored, unsatisfied. Adding another hobby or activity may not give you the sense of productivity you crave. You won't feel important to others. You can fill your life with recreational activities, watching television, and taking care of your own matters, but it won't be enough.

Without your need for productivity being met and without a feeling of being necessary in the lives of others, you may begin to punish your body. You may hurt yourself by overexercising, dieting to an extreme, or paying inordinate attention to your physical appearance.

Mary was one such woman. The wife of a prominent local businessman, she lived in a mansion on a hill. With her teenage children away at boarding school, Mary was left with empty days and nights. Though her care for her children had been meager to begin with, now she was left with nothing at all to divert her attention. At a friend's suggestion, she began playing golf. What began as a pleasant way to spend an afternoon became an obsession that had her on the golf course eight hours a day, seven days a week.

Mary also became consumed with her appearance. She had extensive plastic surgery, bought a new wardrobe, and continued to play golf. Mary was busy. Mary was active. But Mary did not feel *necessary* anywhere. It is God's will that we touch this world with his love. Mary did not reach out. She merely improved her game.

Mary worked harder than ever on her game. She began suffering injuries. First the shoulder, then the wrist. She caught a flu that had her in bed for six weeks. She was frustrated and unhappy. And she thought it was because she couldn't play golf for awhile. She still ignored her deepest needs.

Recreation is good, and we need recreation, as well as work. But when it takes the place of all else, the soul cries out from a sense of loss. We *need* to do things for others. We need to feel we are necessary. Nobody will do it for us. We are responsible ourselves for identifying and fulfilling this need.

Your body is precious to God. It was given to you as a temple of the Holy Spirit. It is a privilege to care for the body and to give it back to God for his purpose. The human body was formed by God for his glory. Illness and trials may befall us, but through all our experiences, God loves our bodies.

GOD SPEAKS:

And you, my little bird,
        I call out of the place
        of emptiness.
I fill you.
Soar higher, sing sweeter,
        and kiss the world
        with my love.

Trust me
        and you will not be
        afraid.
Trust me
        and you will stop
        hurting yourself.
Trust me
  and you will know
  you are safe
  even when it appears
  you are not.
Trust me
        and in time
        you will grow to love
        my discipline.

Based on JAMES 2:24

10

The Dynamic of Multiplication

∞

The principle of divine multiplication is based on the creativity of God. By acts of his own creative power, the Lord multiplies himself and the fruit of his Spirit within us. When we enter into our God-blessed creativity, we in essence join him in the creation of the world. That world is the world of faith. Of hope. Of love.

The biblical miracles that best demonstrate the scope and magnificence of the principle of multiplication are found in all four Gospels, referred to twice in Matthew and Mark, making six references in all. Here's Matthew's account:

As evening approached, the disciples came to him and said, "This is a remote place, and it's already getting late. Send the crowds away, so they can go to the villages and buy themselves some food."

Jesus replied, "They do not need to go away. You give them something to eat."

"We have here only five loaves of bread and two fish," they answered.

"Bring them here to me," he said. And he directed the people to sit down on the grass. Taking the five loaves and the two fish and looking up to heaven, he gave thanks and broke the loaves. Then he gave them to the disciples, and the disciples gave them to the people.

They all ate and were satisfied, and the disciples picked up twelve basketfuls of broken pieces that were left over. The number of those who ate was about five thousand men, besides women and children.   MATTHEW 14:15-21

When we're tired and hungry and it looks as if there's nothing around to nourish us, where do we turn? Our miracle-working God is always ready to display his compassion and mercy toward us. He longs to feed us from his own heart. We can turn to him.

Share the Miracle

The first thing we should observe about this outstanding miracle is the involvement of the disciples in the act. Jesus says to the disciples, *"You* give the people something to eat." (He already knows the disciples have nothing to feed them and not enough money to buy food.)

The Lord himself had all the knowledge and power necessary to multiply the food, but he loves to involve us in his miracles. He says to us, *"You* go into all the world preaching the gospel." He says, *"You* will do greater works than I do." He says, "*You* bring the loaves and fishes to me." By our own love and trust in him, the goodness and love of God are multiplied. The disciples didn't argue or balk; they obediently carried out the Lord's instructions. They *trusted* Jesus.

A little boy had a lunch of five loaves and two fishes, a couple of flat fish sandwiches, actually. The Lord used the boy's generosity and the disciples' obedience to multiply more than food.

Faith was multiplied.

Love of God was multiplied.

Joy was multiplied.

Thankfulness was multiplied.

The miracle unfolds. Jesus directed the people to sit around him on the grass in companies of fifties. There was no confusion among so many people. All was orderly. The people didn't rush Jesus like packs of starving dogs. They sat in orderly, manageable units awaiting their miracle meal. What does this say about us when we are clamoring for a miracle? God speaks in a still, small voice. While clamoring and frantic, we can't hear him.

In keeping with Eastern custom, the five thousand men sat apart. Only the men were counted, so I imagine that there were probably at least twice that number of people, with the addition of the tally of women and children.

Jesus gave thanks. Then he broke the bread with his hands. The Jewish loaves were hard and about a finger's width thick. The multiplication of the food took place in his hands.

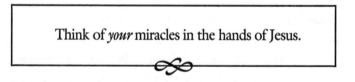

Think of *your* miracles in the hands of Jesus.

Jesus broke the pieces of bread and kept on breaking the pieces of bread. They multiplied and kept on multiplying. The law of multiplication goes on and on until there is more of the blessing than we can consume at once.

Was it "too much of a good thing"? I don't think so. There is no excess in God's kingdom. There is abundance but no leftovers to go unused. There were twelve basketfuls left after all the people had been fed. That's one for each disciple to take home. The workman is worthy of her or his hire.

Who actually *fed* the people? Who carried the food to the people? The disciples. "*You* feed them," Jesus had said.

We are not called to be onlookers when it comes to God's miracles. We are not called to be tellers of the Word only, but doers and partakers of the Word as well. We can multiply the fruit of our beautiful souls each day. When the Dynamic of Love possesses our souls, it multiplies. Each act of faith we engage in inspires another and another until our faith multiplies to soaring heights.

Paul wrote to the Thessalonians, "We ... thank God for you ... because your faith is growing more and more, and the love every one of you has for each other is increasing" (2 Thes 1:3).

We multiply our faith with every thought and act of faith. We multiply our love with each thought and act of love. And that's a miracle.

God multiplies our "I Cans." Jesus' disciples must have been vexed and worried before the meal that day. They had sat with him for hours as he taught the people on the side of a hill. They, too, must have been very hungry. When Jesus told them to feed the people, the disciples must have shaken their heads wondering how in the world such a big order could be fulfilled. Over five thousand hungry people and only a couple of fish sandwiches to go around.

But when the disciples entered into the miracle with the Lord, every "I Can't" became an *"I Can."*

"I Cans" multiply rapidly. You will find new thoughts, his thoughts, tumbling from your lips. You will discover the old self-sabotaging self-talk diminishing and renewed thoughts taking precedence.

Something else comes into focus at this point. It is the awareness and acceptance of which ones of the "I Can'ts" are actually realistic. It is important to the health of your heart and soul to no longer be afraid of what you do not or cannot do. We need to accept and appreciate our limitations if we are to be truly confident, dynamic women of God. This may seem like a contradiction, but it is a crucial factor. Reread Key #4, the Dynamic of Courage.

What are we multiplying? In the play *Happy Days*, by Samuel Beckett, the main character, Winnie, performs the entire play from a hole in a dirt mound. We see only half of her body poking out of the hole for the first act. By the second act, only her head can be seen. Throughout the play she repeats, "Oh, this is a happy day!"

This is a two-character play, with Willie, Winnie's husband, appearing intermittently and responding only occasionally to Winnie's long monologue. The knowledge of his presence is a source of comfort and inspiration to Winnie, the delight of her "happy days."

Winnie merrily talks about her life and life in general while inspecting objects in her purse. At one point she takes up a toothbrush and examines the handle through a glass. "Fully guaranteed,..." she reads, "genuine pure ..." She peers again. "Genuine pure ... hog's setae." Delighted, she removes her glasses and says, "That is what I find so wonderful, that not a day goes by—hardly a day without some addition to one's knowledge."

The play reduces life to a microscopic level where things like shade and sun, a toothbrush, a mirror, a parasol, a handkerchief, a breeze, the memory of a song, are all major characters in life's scenario. And though Winnie is sinking further and further into her hole, she repeats, "Oh, this is a happy day!"

A psychological interpretation of this play might be that Winnie is in denial. Winnie is talking pure hogwash and can't see it. At the end of the play, embedded up to her neck and capable of moving only her eyes, she sees her husband crawling around on the mound and sighs, "Oh, this *is* a happy day."

The literary evaluation of the play would call it a "harsh search for the meaning of existence while probing relationships that bind one person to another."

Spiritually, the play demonstrates a Lazarus who is only half dead. Slowly the tomb consumes Lazarus until he can move nothing at all. He has lost himself. He is dead, but not quite. What good are the joys of life, the happy days, if one is spiritually dead? What good are my hands, my eyes, if I am spiritually bereft?

The relentless shining of the sun in this play reminds me of the singing of the birds in the "Fable of the Woman and Her View," the "too-much-of-a-good-thing" syndrome. It takes a person who is fully developed spiritually to appreciate heaven on earth, to really grasp and hold on to Jesus' words, "I have come to give you life and to give it to you more abundantly."

The Dynamic Key of Multiplication is one of the most valuable and important principles we can learn. The person you are within, how you think, how you enter your solitude, where you place your loves—all multiply with use.

Lazarus, dead in the tomb, could multiply nothing but death. In the Beckett play, Winnie multiplied only the fruitless act of enduring while browsing through life.

Multiply your beautiful thoughts. Every beautiful and true thought opens the pathway for more of the same. We should think of ourselves as in training. Our thought lives are getting more and more skilled. Every time you recognize a misbelief and replace it with the truth, you reinforce the renewed mind. When you make a habit of trying to understand all of your emotions, including those of the shadowy side, you are multiplying your self-understanding. You are taking steps toward loving God with a purer heart. You are blessing your own soul.

If I am to bless the Lord with my soul, I must look at my soul and see what exactly it is I am giving to God. My soul, the lovely calm pool of my truest self, given up to God as a sweet love offering, doesn't develop itself overnight. With the constant input of the Word of God, the continual refusal to stain my soul with the murky drippings of the world, and my habitual celebrating of Christ's love for me, my soul will flower.

Habits that multiply. A habit is defined as the "prevailing disposition or character of a person's thoughts and feelings." Inner habits are the forces propelling us forward or backward. It's not your outward habits of swearing, smoking, drinking, overeating, or gossiping that multiply themselves as much as what you *tell* yourself about these actions. We respond to what we believe.

The habitual lie, "This won't hurt me," spoken while we engage in a destructive behavior, is born of another lie in our inner dialogue that we have already discussed—the "I'm not worth much" mentality. Where do these misbeliefs originate? In our thoughts. Somewhere in our lives we believed it was okay to think this way and the thoughts multiplied.

I can't multiply God's love for me if I don't receive it. I can't multiply who I am in Christ if I can't hear what he tells me. I can't multiply the goodness I receive along my life's path if I have no idea where I'm going or for what purpose.

My lack of confidence multiplies until I've got one foot in the tomb, like Winnie in the Beckett play. Jesus may be calling my name, but I've built a habit of not listening to him. If I've built a habit of only being in tune with the shadow side, it's the shadow side I feed, not my spiritual side, not the bright side where Jesus stands in the sun calling, "Come forth!"

The Examined Heart

Lift up your heart to God for his blessed, examining touch. He looks into your heart. He loves your soul. He wants the "I Can'ts" destroyed. He answers when you pray,

Search me, O God, and know my heart;
test me and know my anxious thoughts.
See if there is any offensive way in me,
and lead me in the way everlasting.   PSALMS 139:23-24

You have the assurance that your personal welfare is burrowed into the center of God's thoughts. David begins Psalm 139 by exclaiming his awareness of the ever-watchful eye of God in his inner life as well as his outward actions:

O Lord, you have searched me
and you know me.
You know when I sit and when I rise;
you perceive my thoughts from afar.
You discern my going out and my lying down;
you are familiar with all my ways.
Before a word is on my tongue
you know it completely, O Lord.

You hem me in—behind and before;
you have laid your hand upon me.
Such knowledge is too wonderful for me,
too lofty for me to attain.   PSALMS 139:1-6

Notice David's sigh of wonder: "Such knowledge is too wonderful for me, too lofty for me to attain." David was thrilled and
mystified by the loving presence of God. We should be. It is
knowledge too lofty for any of us to attain. We don't have to
understand it, but we do need to be aware that our souls are valuable to God.

Multiplying your weaknesses. If you know you have a strong
desire to please people, to make everybody happy even at your
own expense, this urge will multiply. If you are in business, your
business will suffer because emotionally you won't be able to successfully employ the professional business tactics that are necessary
for turning a profit. Know your weaknesses and your "I Can'ts."
Recognize them because they will multiply unless you change
them to "I Cans."

If you are afraid of failure, or if you are bent on proving yourself
to the world, you will multiply fear instead of faith. You can't hide
your "I Can'ts" under the rug or under a cash register. Eventually
they poke their little heads out and take a bite out of you. And
they will keep on biting. You'll subsequently hurt yourself in many
ways. One of the most common is to be busy earning the approval
of the world (which you never get enough of) while pushing away
the people closest to you. Your unhappiness will only multiply
itself.

If you see the world around you as a big, bad, and terrible place,
with the mistaken idea that it's cruel and unmanageable, you will

sabotage yourself at every turn. School, work, play, and love will all eventually prove too big for you to handle, and your nervousness, fear, and worry will multiply.

Think of yourself as an "I Can" woman, multiplying "I Cans" at every turn in your life. You can rise up, like Lazarus, shedding the rags of old fears and needs for approval. The world isn't too big for you to manage.

Multiply Your "I Cans"

Jesus is saying to you, "Here's the miracle. Now you permit it to multiply." If you will look closely at your life you will see how his goodness is multiplied daily. God is infinitely good. His goodness is boundless, knowing no limits, infinite. He is goodness itself, the supreme endless goodness. One sip of his goodness and you'll never stop thirsting for more. His goodness, which endures forever, will multiply in your life, even as David sang in Psalm 23, "Surely goodness and mercy will follow me all the days of my life." Your *good* God and Savior rescues you daily from defeat and sorrow.

It was a *good* God who miraculously provided for the Israelites in the wilderness. It was a good God who loved and nourished them with heavenly food when they ran out of their food supplies a month and a half after crossing the Red Sea. The goodness of God became their sustenance by providing manna for them to eat. God honored the Dynamic of the Physical Body and fed his children so they would be strong and healthy. God told Moses, "I will rain down bread from heaven," and he did. Morning and night manna fell from heaven after the dew.

The manna filled and nourished the two million Israelites for forty years. I've read that manna had the taste of honey wafers. I've read it changed flavors depending on how it was cooked. The Israelites learned to bake it into cakes that tasted like "cakes baked with oil" (Ex 16:23). There was only one rule they had to strictly follow. God ordered that they take what was necessary for each day and no more. Any unused leftovers would spoil and smell terrible.

God provided the miracle, and his people administered its benefits. It's a wonderful example of the law of multiplication. What is your manna? Can it multiply day and night for the next forty years as you journey through life?

The answer is yes. You can go on with the Dynamic of Confidence as you multiply your faith and blessings. Join with your sisters across the globe, taking your rightful place in the kingdom of God.

We women live in God's heart of hearts, and like Mary, the mother of Jesus, we can sing,

> My soul praises the Lord
> and my spirit rejoices in God my Savior,
> for he has been mindful
> of the humble state of his servant....
> He ... has lifted up the humble.
> He has filled the hungry
> with good things.   LUKE 1:46,47; 52,53

Conclusion

The Confident and Dynamic You

∞

In this final chapter I want to look at how the Ten Keys to confident and dynamic living affect our relationships. The quality of our relationships with others depends upon having all ten of the keys presented in this book in place in our lives.

Let's first look at our feelings and how we manage them. Do we understand our feelings?

Feelings Are Important

A very big problem among women is a natural inclination to deny bad feelings. "I'm not angry, I'm just *hurt*," we'll say, while inside we may be seething. Or when we've been offended or abused in some way, we say, "Oh, that's OK—I don't mind," when we really *do* mind very much.

This denial of our feelings then seeps into our expectations of others. A loved one will tell us he is angry, and we automatically respond with, "Oh, but you shouldn't be angry." A friend confides she's feeling miserably depressed, and we bounce back with, "How can you be depressed with so many blessings in your life?" A daughter or son complains of positively hating someone at school,

187

and we immediately spout out with, "Now, now, Honey. Jesus loves *everyone*."

A woman tells me, "More than anything, I want to be a model mother." She wants to be a sterling example of self-discipline and godliness to help form her daughters' attitudes toward God and life. My response is to wonder if trying to spare our children from ever seeing the trials we suffer is the best way of teaching them.

When your children see you overcome a bad temper or a bad habit—or when they see you handling a negative situation with grace—these are memories that become fixed in their hearts. These are examples they will remember.

Are you safe to talk to? I raised two daughters by myself. In looking back, I know now that there were times when it was not safe for them to talk to me openly. Though I knew better, I would try to talk my children out of their feelings if they were negative or unpleasant. I would argue, "Oh, no, you don't *really* feel that way," or perhaps I would remind them of the message we heard the pastor preach last Sunday. But many times I didn't listen and respond in a way that said, *"I hear you. What you are feeling and thinking is important. You are worth hearing from, even if I don't agree with you."*

I needed the Dynamic of Love and the Dynamic of Fullness in operation at those times. I had to realize God didn't give me children so I could push them into a mold formed by *me* and *my* ideas. With the Dynamic of Solitude we can be still and listen to what God has to say about our loved ones. How is he directing us? How is he speaking to them?

When we are at variance with our loved ones, words we need to repeat often at home are "I respect you even though we may think differently and hold different opinions." There are many ways to show love, and the Dynamic of Love taught me that all the love I would ever feel in my life would have to come from the place within where first God had spoken his love to me. My only understanding of true love is from his perspective.

In order to help build strong character in myself and my children, I had to understand that one of the most valuable character-building tools is respect. I had to learn to stop trying to talk myself and others out of legitimate feelings.

If you have a teenager, can he or she feel safe enough to confide in you about the new conflicts that he or she is confronted with? Is it *safe* to talk to you?

Do you still punish others for being open with you? Suppose your child disobeys you. The child confesses that she has committed some violation of the family rules. Do you roar with indignation, impose a severe punishment, shame the child?

Suppose that instead you react with, "I appreciate your honesty. It builds trust between us when you tell me the truth. However, you did break your promise to follow such-and-such a rule, and it's an important one." From that point, you could enforce the appropriate discipline.

Discipline is quite different from punishment. Discipline is meant to teach, to guide, to instruct and build us up. It comes from the word "disciple." Punishment, on the other hand, is merely an imposed penalty.

How much better to allow our children, friends, and coworkers to express feelings even if they are negative. We each have the right to forge our own path in the world, even though our mistakes may flutter about us like leaves in autumn. As long as the feelings are not accusing, demanding, or condemning, they need to be expressed and heard.

When I consider James 5:11, "The Lord is full of compassion

and mercy," I see that God is fully aware of our human condition. He is aware of our natural tendency to panic, to be judgmental, to insist the world be run our way.

If a child or a friend confides something that you find disagreeable, do you rise up in indignation ready to reprove and correct? Or do you listen and *discuss* the matter? Sometimes the wisest thing you can do is be quiet, say nothing, and listen. That's what the tender heart does. It was born in solitude, built on love and hope. It is creative and unafraid. It is the heart of a grown-up. It is the confident woman's heart.

Understanding your feelings. Your feelings not only need to be listened to, they need to be examined. What messages are you giving yourself when you feel bad? If you are flooded over with worries about bills, pressures at work, a disagreement with someone, a disappointment, or the former marriage that still haunts you, recognize these feelings. Remember what we learned in Key #6, the Dynamic of Confidence. Try to evaluate what you think about every day, especially when you are alone.

Don't ever be content with accepting bad feelings and thoughts by ignoring their underlying messages. If you are hurting, your soul is signaling for your attention.

My friend Christina tells me that for years she had excused her bad temper by blaming it on her Italian heritage. Her kids grew up believing all Italians were born angry and volatile. Of course my friend was lying to herself and everyone else by making excuses for not listening to what was *really* going on inside her heart. She could not conquer her temper by talking herself out of her feelings. Words like "Don't be angry; it's not ladylike" didn't change her.

Something inside her was crying out for attention. What messages was she giving herself? Here's where we go back to the Key of Solitude, and we embrace the Key of Fullness, as well. Christina had to learn to say things to herself like,

"I'm feeling angry, so what is it that I am really reacting to?"

"What is this situation really saying to me?"

"What am I telling myself in my thought life?"

For Christina, *fear* was her major culprit. Christina was very frightened of the shadow side of her personality. She feared that any day she would pop, explode. She feared she wasn't really a nice person at all. The worse she felt, the more angry she acted. She developed a cycle of guilt and deceit and self-disgust.

If I feel something unacceptable and sinful like envy, jealousy, prejudice, or anger, and I don't dare face what's going on inside me, I'll lie about it. A cycle of deceit and guilt is hard to break. It's necessary to learn to evaluate our feelings and to figure out what the "trigger" was. We might be able to see, for example:

"The reason I feel like screaming and punching the wall is because people don't do things the way I want them to."

"The reason I feel like bingeing on chocolate cake and fudge ice cream is because I am feeling alone and afraid of people right now. I want something to fill my life with sweetness and make me feel good."

Even though we know we should, we don't always turn to the Word of God immediately when we are hurting and feeling fearful. We forget that he, God himself, understands and loves us.

"I understand." Recently I walked into a university classroom I thought was empty. A young man stood in the corner, his face red and his body bent over. I thought he was ill, but then suddenly he lunged forward and punched the wall with a blow of his fist, crying out, "She never *listens* to me!" Then I realized that the girl who had just whisked past me in the hall must have been his girlfriend. I suspected they had just had an argument, and I just happened to catch him at an intensely emotional moment when he thought no one was around. He stood trembling, holding his bloodied knuckles and poised to punch the wall again. Then he caught sight of me.

What do you say to someone who is hurting himself? "Hey, nobody's worth breaking your fingers over"; or, "Come on, fella, snap out of it!"; or, "If life hands you a lemon, make lemonade"; or, "What are you, crazy? Don't ruin your writing hand!"

Students would soon be entering the classroom. So I said quietly, "I'm sorry she didn't listen to you."

He squinted his eyes at me, sighed, and after a long pause mumbled, "Yeah, well, she never listens.... It's nothing new."

"I understand," I said.

He broke into an embarrassed smile. He seemed to calm down. "Yeah?"

"I understand," I repeated.

Just those two quiet words calmed him. His face relaxed. His shoulders slumped. People began pouring into the classroom and taking their seats. The young man picked up his books with his good hand, nodded at me, and as he left the room, turned and said, "Hey—thanks."

I understand are magic words to our ears. We hunger for understanding. We desperately want to be heard, known, listened to. Add the magic words "I understand" to your vocabulary and you will multiply the best in yourself and others. You will open the path to awareness and compassion.

Comforting words like "I can see you're angry" or "I'm sorry such-and-such happened" can be like a balm to the upset person. These are the words we want to hear. At times of intense distress we don't need reprimanding or correction. We need understanding.

Beautiful words: I respect your feelings. I see altogether too much unhappiness resulting from unmet demands and expectations. To respect another person's feelings is freeing.

The words "I respect your feelings" are important to add to your vocabulary. Also important:

"I respect your *thinking*."

"I respect your *honesty*."

"I respect *you*."

Avoid the expressions that end with what I call the "caboose clause" that begins with *but*:

"I respect your feelings, *but* they're really dumb."

"I respect your thoughts, *but* I don't know how you can think that way."

"I respect your honesty, *but* now I'm really going to punish you for it."

Respecting your own feelings. It takes the Dynamic of Courage to express our own feelings openly. If we lack courage, here's what we do when we try to talk ourselves out of our feelings. We say things like:

"No, I don't feel angry. I'm just tired, that's all,"

"Hey, if I break my hand by hitting the wall, it's not my fault. I inherited wall-punching from my dad."

"No, I'm not worried. What do I care if I get evicted from my home?"

"Fear? Me? Never."

We excuse bad behavior with some lie about not feeling well or being overworked and stressed. These lies are saying, "I lack courage to face how I really feel. I lack courage to admit my feelings to myself, so how can I express them to you?" These examples of an underlying lack of courage *always* make for problems in relationships.

If we can't express our feelings in an open way, we feel misunderstood and frustrated. This leads to either hiding our feelings or being deceitful and pretending we're feeling and thinking what we are not. Kids are great at the latter. "How are you, dear?" asks the parent. "Fine," snaps the daughter as she goes on her way. In truth she may be battling some very difficult problem or situation.

You Can Do It!

Stacey was a woman who believed the world was too big for her to manage. Outwardly she seemed confident and self-assured, but inwardly she was deeply insecure. She returned to college after her divorce, but quit when it became obvious that going to school included not only hard work and concentrated effort but a certain amount of competition and stress. She started a new job and quit after three months. There was too much to learn; it was too difficult and stressful. She began working for the temporary agencies just to make her bread and butter, but often didn't show up for the jobs she was assigned. Too scary.

After several counseling sessions, Stacey finally admitted her fear of a world around her that was just too big for her to manage. She had gotten by on her good looks for most of her life. Men had paid her way. First boyfriends, then husbands. But relationships were hard for her to maintain. She never felt worthy. She compared herself to other women who she believed were, for the most part, smarter, better adjusted, more clever than she.

Stacey believed school was easier for others than for her. She believed returning to the workforce was easier for other women than for her. She believed other people had it much better.

One day Stacey said to me, "I could never do what you do."

"Oh?" I said. "What do you mean?"

"Well, you're not afraid of anything."

I could have laughed out loud. "Stacey," I said as calmly as I could, "confidence is a skill we teach ourselves. Nobody comes by it naturally. It's gained by discipline and taking our relationship with God seriously." I went on to tell her how I had once had an inferiority complex the size of Chicago, including its suburbs. The world is a very scary place to a woman who has not learned the

Ten Keys of dynamic life I have shared with you in this book. I had to learn to tell myself the truth about myself and the world around me. So did Stacey.

She began by examining the damaging words she told herself every day. "I can't" was right up there at the top.

Stacey had to begin by replacing "I can't" with the truth, which was:

"Though it appears to me that I am helpless and can't face (whatever), I *can* do it."

"I am alive, therefore I am not helpless."

Throughout the Bible are the stories of men and women who didn't feel worthy of carrying on a particular task God required of them. Moses argued he wasn't presentable enough when God called him to approach the pharaoh. Moses said, "I can't! I stutter. I just can't!" But God knew Moses better than Moses knew himself.

Sarah, Elijah, Jeremiah, Jonah, Ruth, Esther . . . all of these great heroes and heroines of the faith had fears they had to overcome. Look at David, who spent much of his life running from King Saul. Was that fun? Here was the boy who had been a hero, having slain the giant Goliath, and what happened after such a feat? He spent years living and hiding in caves like an animal running from a hunter.

If the world seems too big to you, take some small steps into what seems impossible or very difficult. After every step you take, say to yourself, "Good for me."

Lazarus came out of the tomb of death one step at a time. He didn't fly out like a bird. He took steps.

Mother's influence. One of the most surprising responses I received on the "For Women Only" survey was to the question, "What women have been the most negative influences on your life?"

Seventy-five percent of the responses came back, "My mother."

Because the survey was anonymous, the women could be completely open and honest, and the explanations were lengthy and pain-filled. The events in these women's lives have multiplied more pain and will go on multiplying until the past is dealt with.

Don't forget, we respond emotionally to events in our lives according to what we *tell* ourselves about these events. We can continue to multiply thoughts such as:

"Life is terrible."

"My mother hurt me so badly I'll never function properly."

"I can forgive but I can't ever, ever forget" (which means I'll go on hurting).

"No one will ever love me."

All of the above are untruths. In order to change them, we need to replace them with new self-talk such as:

"Though my life has been difficult and I've suffered, I *can* go on learning the skills of confidence. I *can* bring joy into my life."

"It's true my mother hurt me with her behaviors, actions, attitudes, words. However, I am a worthwhile woman of God. David said in Psalm 27, 'Though my father and *mother* forsake me, the Lord will receive me.'"

"The Lord is both my father and mother."

"Maybe I feel unlovable, but these thoughts stain my soul. What I am really saying is, 'I'm afraid of love.'"

"I choose to be open to love and beauty in my life. Surely goodness and mercy are following me all the days of my life. God has said, 'Never will I leave you; never will I forsake you.'"

The Lazarus Woman of Tomorrow

Together we can change our world. We can climb out of our grave clothes—past hurts and failures—and enter our new confident and dynamic life with pride and dignity.

I envision tomorrow's Lazarus Woman as a woman who is unafraid, courageous, dynamic. I see her as a woman of hope, who is unafraid to achieve great things for the glory of God. I see a confident Lazarus Woman, a woman who is not fettered by the past but strengthened by it. I see a kind and merciful woman who loves deeply and truly, whose center of being is found in solitude alone with her God. I see a wise, understanding, strong woman. I see her multiplying her goodness and beauty everywhere she goes.

I see the Lazarus Woman. I see *you*.

For Women Only— A Questionnaire

Now that you have finished reading the book, this questionnaire is for your own personal use and self-discovery. Use it in your Bible study for discussion, as well as in your private moments alone with God.

Please answer the following questions with as much honesty and thought as possible.

1. When do you feel the *most* brave, courageous? (Take your time with this one. Give circumstances. Use an extra sheet of paper if necessary).

2. When do you feel the *least* brave and courageous? (Give circumstances.)

3. Do you have goals in your life?_____ List the most relevant:

4. When do you stop yourself from reaching your goals?

5. When you look at your life, can you say it's been 100-percent fulfilling?_____

Give reasons for why or why not:

7. Has God ever disappointed you? Explain.

8. When do you feel closest to God?

9. Do you believe in relationships with others that love is something that must be earned? _____

10. Have you worked hard to earn love in your life? _____ How have you done this?

11. Do you feel you have enough love from others in your life now?_____
    Explain:

12. When do you feel the *most* lovable?

13. Do you think women should be leaders in society, church, politics, and community? _____
    Why or why not?

14. Do you see yourself as a strong, capable, and courageous woman?____
    Why or why not?

15. What women have been the most *negative* influences on your life?

16. Describe these women:

17. Have you overcome these negative influences? If so, how?

18. Name some women you *admire* and hold as role models in your life.

    What qualities do they possess that you admire and wish to aspire to?

19. If you could be anyone in the world, whom would you choose to be?

20. Why did you choose this person?

21. What do you need to do to be more brave and courageous in your life?

Women of Confidence

SERIES

The Women of Confidence Series is designed to help women confidently express their God-given gifts in every facet of their intellect, personality, style, and talents. All women have things they wish they could do better—or do at all. Those things may be something practical and close to home—like learning to communicate or to entertain. Or they could be something to fortify the soul—like praying. From helping women define personal goals and build strong relationships, to learning how to communicate and deepen their spirituality, this series has it all.

Written by respected Christian communicators and authors, the Women of Confidence Series helps women find new ways to live enthusiastically and confidently in the light of God's love.

Also available:

A Woman of Strength

Reclaim Your Past, Seize Your Present, and Secure Your Future

NEVA COYLE

In *A Woman of Strength*, Neva Coyle helps readers to redeem their pain, and redirect their focus to meet the challenges of life with grace and courage. Through stories of women who discovered their own strength, the author shows us that the present is an opportunity to heal from the past, and that the future can be exciting territory to explore with confidence. *$10.99*

Available at your local Christian bookstore.